THE RFP ALTERNATIVE

Technology Purchasing Redefined

DENIS P. O'DONOVAN, JR.

HERE IS WHAT PEOPLE ARE SAYING...

"I.T. Leadership should absolutely leverage Denis O'Donovan's experience, passion, and acumen to simplify the process of sourcing technology, communications, and network services for enterprises. Rarely have I experienced the exceptional combination of industry knowledge and the drive to fight for the betterment of his customer's technology roadmap, and it has been an honor to work alongside Mr. O'Donovan in that pursuit for the past decade."

—Mason Miles, Executive Vice President Sales
for CommandLink – ProfitComm vendor

"I have been working with Denis for over 7 years and across multiple platforms. He is the only person I work with for any technology needs we have at our company. He is always available and willing to navigate through the various bureaucracy and fix any issues we have encountered. I could not do what I do without having him as a trusted partner."

—Ladan Rykiel -Managing Partner -Orthopedic
Billing Consultants

"Using ProfitComm's RFP Alternative process takes every pain point away from ordering technology solutions. I simply let them know what criteria I require and a few days later (sometimes a few hours!) I have a plethora of vendor options to choose from to suit my needs. Their process is truly the Easy Button for ordering Technology Solutions!"

—Mike Bullock – IT Manager and customer for 15+ years

"The vendor agnostic approach makes sourcing vendors easy and more efficient. Getting right to the point and providing like for like comparison saves us time in our decision-making process. Less meetings, less back and forth with multiple sales teams is appreciated."

—Frank Lighty – Network Manager - KCI Technologies

CONTENTS

FOREWORD

by Mr. Ben Humphreys,
owner of Comtel Communications and Simplicity
VOIP and a well-respected industry expert

On a winter afternoon in 1999, I received a phone call from my channel sales manager at LCI International. She mentioned that she had interviewed an incredible individual that I should speak with to join my firm as a sales consultant. She was not one to offer this type of recommendation lightly, so my curiosity was piqued. Little did I know that the call would lead to a 23-year business relationship and friendship. When I first spoke to Denis, I was impressed with his fire and determination but more importantly with his sense of values and work ethic. In my mind, he was the total package, and he would be just what my fledgling organization needed to move to the next level.

Over the years, Denis has worked with countless clients. He truly places the customer's interest first and delivers analytical approach to his clients. "Client first" means something to Denis - it's easy to say that but I have numerous stories, and one immediately comes to mind. We shared a mutual client that was running a call center for a major cosmetic company. Their VoIP provider was experiencing serious problems on Black Friday. Undaunted, Denis rolled up his sleeves and jumped in. During that holiday weekend, we were able to escalate getting executive attention on the situation that helped resolve the client problem.

In this book, Denis takes the reader on a journey to understand the current state of the RFP process, his solution to modernize it, and make it stronger in 2022 and beyond. He does an excellent job of laying out pitfalls in the RFP process and provides real life examples that decisionmakers face daily. Some of this will surprise you and some things will make you laugh. The RFP Alternative process that he proposes takes an old standard and moves it forward. His advocacy and the advocacy of his peers will show a new way forward for technology procurement that will stand the test of time.

INTRODUCTION

"The world is changing so fast that the future
goes past as soon as the present."
— Anuj

Just about every category of technology has evolved like crazy in the last forty years. If you're old enough to have lived through those changes, then you've seen firsthand how profoundly they have impacted our everyday lives.

At the time of this writing, I'm fifty-one years old. When I graduated high school in 1988, I didn't have a cell phone, and the internet didn't exist for anyone outside of perhaps the US government and certain research colleges. There was no email and no text messaging, so if I wanted to get hold of a friend, I used a rotary dial landline phone with a cord. However, my friend had to be physically present where the other phone was located in order to answer the call. If I called him at home while he was hanging out at the mall, I was out of luck.

Of course, if I couldn't reach my friend by phone, I could write him a letter and send it via snail mail, though it would take him a day or two to get it. If neither of these options worked, I could always go see my friend in person and hope he was at home when I got there.

That's just the way it was in those days. It may seem shocking to young people now, but sometimes you just couldn't get hold of people.

Road trips were a much different affair back then, as well. We had no GPS service, so when we set out on a long drive, we used this ancient technology called paper maps. They came in book form or as big fold-outs, and they were produced by companies like Rand McNally and Atlas. Most gas stations had big rotating display stands containing local, regional, and national maps, which was really convenient if you got lost on your way to Grandma's house, or Disney World, or the Grand Canyon, or wherever you happened to be going.

All of the tech that didn't exist when I was eighteen years old is now deeply woven into the fabric of our everyday lives. We text, email, browse the internet, call people around the world, shop online, and use GPS services routinely, without even thinking about how amazing it is. In 1988, I left home for a week during Senior Week in Ocean City, MD. My parents didn't know if I was alive or dead for seven whole days. Today we have Life360, so we can know where our kids are 24/7. Stalking our kids has become a daily occurrence.

Some of the things we're able to do now would have been inconceivable to me in high school. Heck, when I started my company   in 1999, long-distance phone service was still a $160 billion-dollar industry. Who pays for long distance phone service anymore? Who would put up with being charged by the minute for calling a family member in another state?

Our daily lives are so much different now than they were when I was eighteen. From ecommerce to remote work to online banking to digital analytics, the tech that touches every aspect of our work and personal lives has changed radically. And yet there's one aspect of doing business that has hardly changed at all: *requests for proposal.*

The way companies announce projects and solicit bids from contractors works pretty much the same now as it did forty years ago. While the whole world has changed around it, RFPs are firmly stuck in the past.

There Must Be a Better Way

Of course, we're all familiar with the way RFPs work. It's what you do when you want to upgrade or install new technology in your company.

Let's suppose you need to upgrade your network. How do you go about doing that? First, the procurement department meets with the IT team and other groups in order to figure out the scope of the work. They craft the scope of the work in a way that presents the existing landscape, identifying the older technology that you already have (e.g., "Baltimore Gas and Electric operates a data network that looks like this…").

Then they describe the state that you want to move toward, identifying all of the physical attributes, including location, quantity, size, speed, and so on (e.g., "We need a hundred cages in the data center to support our infrastructure, and that will require X amount of power, with X amount of bandwidth and storage."). There's a bit of a guessing game here, because you have to give your best estimate about what you're going to need to support you a few years into the future, taking into account the rate of change in your industry, historical data, company growth rates, etc.

Putting all of this information together in a document might take anywhere from six to nine months and require input from multiple teams. In the end, you will have an RFP document that is very lengthy, typically over 100 pages. Once the RFP is complete, it is sent out into the world, published to a public forum, so vendors can bid on it.

Typically, a vendor will print the enormous document and take some time to read it. There's usually an opportunity for them to ask questions after a certain period of time during a pre-bid meeting.

After a lengthy Q & A, vendors send in their submissions to bid on the project. The procurement department and IT staff then have the unenviable job of reading every single proposal from vendors. Whether they get thirty proposals or 230, they have to read them all and deduce which vendors can meet your needs.

From there, they usually create a short list of potential vendors, perhaps ten to twelve, and schedule face-to-face meetings with them, where they ask questions like, "Why are you the best candidate for this project?" After all of these meetings, they whittle down the list again, then conduct additional meetings.

If you've been through it, then you know from experience that it's a long, arduous, and time-consuming process of slowly narrowing the initial list of vendors to get to the winner. When you deal with state or local government vendors, then there's an additional complication: the losing vendors can formally dispute your final selection. Consequently, the organization putting out the RFP has to validate their decision, which involves a whole other process.

There are meetings on top of meetings, calls on top of calls, and through it all, your company has to drive the entire RFP process. In addition to all of that, you still have to take care of your normal, daily work. You can't shut down your business just to get through an RFP process, so that makes it take even longer.

Chances are, the RFP process I've just described is already familiar to you. We've only skimmed the surface, but you've no doubt sat in countless meetings with vendors, spent hours and hours reading through and discussing proposals. In an age when technology has made so many other areas of life and business more flexible and convenient, it's astonishing that we still slog through these long, arduous RFP processes every time we want to solicit bids for a project.

There simply has to be a better way!

Through the RFP Trenches

As it turns out, there is! In the following chapters, I'm going to show you an RFP Alternative process that streamlines the evaluation process by using only people who are extremely well-versed subject matter experts in the relevant segments of technology. By bringing only pre-qualified, pre-vetted vendors to the table, you will eliminate a huge amount of wasted time and effort.

The key is to work with people who understand the market, the vendor landscape and know how to navigate it, so they can negotiate on your behalf. It's also important that they are vendor-neutral, working as advocates for you, the customer, rather than for specific vendors. The end result is an RFP Alternative process that is efficient and effective—a headache-free process that delivers the best and most qualified vendor faster and at a reasonable price.

You might wonder why I'm so passionate about finding a better way to do RFPs. The fact is, I've been in the technology field for twenty-five years, and I've run my own agency since 1999.

But first, please indulge me in a little flashback to the mid-1990s. I had just started a sales position with LCI International, and I was broke. I mean *broke!* I bought a couple of suits and ties with what was left of my credit card limit, and I shlepped off to sell long distance service to Baltimore businesses. Yippee!

In those days, long-distance sales reps were loathed because they were everywhere. Our job was to knock on office doors even if there was a clearly visible "no soliciting" sign. In fact, we saw those offices as a challenge, a test of our selling skills. One time, I went to a place in Baltimore with a sign on the door that said, "Solicitors will be shot on site." Well, I opened the door and crawled on the ground, even though I was in a suit and tie and had my briefcase in hand.

The woman at the front desk looked at me like I had two heads. "What are you doing?" she asked.

"Trying not to get shot," I replied.

My approach worked, and I was allowed to see the boss and make my pitch. I got through to the decision-maker by thinking differently, and I'm happy to report I did not get shot. Of course, I didn't get the deal either, but at least I passed the test. Still, my older self can't believe how obnoxious that little tactic was.

After a month or two at LCI, the starter fried on my red 1988 Mazda RX7, but I wasn't earning commissions yet. Still broke, I did what any other stubborn Irishman would do. I parked on hills, so I could use the slope to start my car. For 3 to 5 more weeks, whenever I went to the office or went knocking on doors, I had to find a steep hill so I could get my car started afterward. I made sure I was the last person in the office at night so no one would see my broke ass pushing my car down the hill.

When I went selling, I usually had to park really far away because business parks tend not to have hills. Just picture a twenty-five-year-old knucklehead in a suit, tie, and wingtips pushing his car down a hill to pop the clutch, knowing that if the car made it to the bottom without starting, he was screwed. Some people celebrate their first commission check with a nice dinner or drinks. I celebrated by getting a new starter.

Eventually, I achieved some success with LCI. Then they were bought by Qwest and began offering more than just long-distance services. That meant more opportunities to offer additional services to businesses. I was able to buy a car with an automatic transmission, and I paid down my credit card debit. More importantly, I began to develop an interest in technology as a long-term career and not just a way to make some money in the present.

The office in Owings Mills, Maryland had numerous direct reps, but one particular office in the corner belonged to the LCI/Qwest channel manager. She supported the agent channel, and I spoke to her often about the business. Those conversations piqued my interest in the consultative side of the company, which set me on the path that got me to where I am today. The channel manager introduced me to Ben Humphreys of Comtel Communications in March of 1999, and that was the beginning of my present course. I was starting from zero so Ben and I agreed on a comp plan that helped me get started under the Comtel brand initially. That and LCI/Qwest stock sales helped me build my business in the basement of a townhouse in Cockeysville, MD without the need for a bank loan or incurring additional personal debt. Ben not only believed in me, but he also invested in me.

It probably makes sense here to outline the different ways vendors get their solutions to the end users. The two ways we will mainly reference are Direct and Indirect, or Channel. Direct reps are employees of the vendor and sell directly to the end user on behalf of the vendor. The vendor pays their salary, their health insurance, commissions, etc… The Channel, or Indirect model, operates independently as Trusted Technology Advisors. In my case my company is ProfitComm and we operate as a Trusted Technology Advisor with a portfolio of over 300 vendors. We are supported by vendor reps, or channel managers. They are direct employees of the vendors, and they are responsible for sales just like Direct Reps, but their process is different in that they market and support companies like ProfitComm and the master agencies, and we bring them opportunities from our marketing efforts.

While I started out in direct sales, I left direct sales to start my own agency in the channel out of sheer frustration that the sales process was *not* customer-centric. Everything was about the transaction, closing the deal, whether it was good for the customer or not. Consequently, customers had to advocate and fight for themselves. It was up to them to educate themselves on all of the technologies that would benefit them so they could spend their money, time, and resources wisely, and they had to do all of this while also keeping up with their day jobs.

I knew there had to be a better way, a customer-centric approach that would help people find the *right* solutions. Indeed, "solutions not sales" resonated strongly with me. After all, let's be honest, in direct sales, you have to sell the deal whether it makes sense for the customer or not because *that's how you feed your family*! You pay the bills to keep the lights on by getting people to buy your employer's tech, and your employer probably has quotas that they expect you to meet.

Since 1999, I have been operating as a vendor-agnostic consultant for my clients. Over the last twenty-plus years, I've probably done more than 300 multi-vendor bids, which enabled me to get the process down to a science. In 2019, I was fortunate enough to be selected to participate in a business owner program at Johns Hopkins called the Goldman Sachs *10,000 Small Business* program.

GS10KSB is an intense, comprehensive program that helps business owners across the country to get better at every facet of their business by developing a growth strategy and building a business plan around it. In the program, I took the shell of what I had been doing for more than twenty years and refined it, making it even better. I incorporated some industry-leading software tools and built out our deliverables.

What had been a behind-the-scenes, between-my-ears, and very vanilla (but effective) process could now be done out in the open. The complex was made simple and delivered to the client's doorstep. We named the process "The RFP Alternative" because our approach to multi-vendor bids was similar to RFPs but offered a process and deliverable to the client that were refreshing alternatives to the old way.

When you're no longer bound by sales or quotas, you can focus solely on driving outcomes for customers. That was my vision for the RFP Alternative, and I've worked hard with my team to refine my better process, one that gets you to the right vendor much, much faster.

I've been in the RFP trenches long enough to see just how cumbersome RFPs can be. In this book, I want to introduce you to a revolutionary new approach. You might be surprised at just how much better it makes the old request for proposal slog!

But first, let's look at the dreaded RFP and see if we can't figure out how the process got so far behind the times in the first place.

xvii

CHAPTER ONE

WHAT IS THE RFP?

"Getting stuck in the past is like guarding a cemetery."
— Hugo Pratt

RFP is technically a three-letter word, but in many organizations, it might as well be a four-letter-word. Everybody hates them. Everybody. I can't think of a single person who loves the way RFPs are done.

So, if we all hate them, why do we keep doing them? Why don't we find a better process, a more streamlined process that gets us to the right solution faster?

In other words, why do we put up with the old RFP process? I think the simple answer is that people don't know there's any other way to do them. "This is how we've always solicited bids for tech upgrades." In the absence of a better solution, organizations default to what they know, and to processes that they believe are tried and true. They simply don't realize there's a new normal.

We touched on this briefly in the introduction, but let's look at the old normal. This should seem familiar to you. It all begins when your company identifies a potential need. Your IT department approaches leadership and says, "Hey, there's some new technology out there that is way better than our current system. We'd better find someone who can transition us to the new tech."

Assuming company leaders agree with this, the next step is to put together an exhaustive analysis of you company's needs from soup to nuts, which means gathering intel about this specific technology, including locations, components, quantities, and so on. You have to clearly identify your needs. Doing this usually involves a procurement officer visiting multiple departments to find out what the needs are, as well as what the new tech could do for them. Is it compatible with other systems you have? Are there expensive integrations that will be undone by the upgrade? Does this affect any contractual terms with other tech that you use?

Then, the need has to be outlined carefully, showing exactly what the need is, where the new tech will go, and what it will mean. It's not uncommon for the growth of a company's infrastructure to outpace the capacity of their technology environment, so let's suppose they have a fiber network with 50 Mbps, and they want to throttle it up to 200 Mbps. In examining the need, they realize they will need a brand-new local access, routers, and a lot of added installation costs. All of this must be carefully outlined. Defining the need in this way can take a very long time, and usually requires input from many different departments.

A good RFP should involve a thorough and honest evaluation of technology needs that leaves a lot of runway for additional and future improvements. In other words, transitioning to new tech should be seen as a journey that will lead to additional growth changes in the future, not a destination. Unfortunately, procurement officers often see an RFP as a one-time transaction to deal with one specific need, so they actually create bigger problems for the company down the road when seeking out new tech.

I've seen far too many examples of companies that spend a ridiculous amount of time and money on upgrading to some new tech only for the solution to be obsolete much sooner than it should. One common way this happens is when they underestimate how much more storage space (or processing power or bandwidth) the company is going to need in the future, so they get locked into solutions (contractually, financially, or otherwise) that they outgrow.

But there's an additional problem. Because RFPs are so time-consuming, some stakeholders simply never get engaged in the process. They have enough on their plates. Indeed, they might not even be aware that an RFP process has begun until it is well under way.

Often it goes something like this. Someone in leadership steps forward and says, "I think we need to migrate to a better call center solution." They haven't talked to the people in the call center about it. They don't bring every stakeholder into the conversation because they don't want to disrupt day-to-day operations. Leaders decide to start an RFP process to find a vendor who will upgrade their call center, and only then do they approach the actual team members in the call center and inform them about it. So, people who should have a voice in outlining the problem and identifying the needs are left out of the conversation until it's too late. This either delays the process or calls for changes mid process to account for modifications.

Once the need has been clearly and exhaustively outlined, some companies create a request for information (RFI), which is a bit like sticking your big toe in a swimming pool to test the water. An RFI is a formal process for collecting information about a possible solution. The company is saying, "Does this make sense for us?" The RFI is pushed out to vendors, and the vendors eventually send their responses. However, this is only a process for gathering general information about potential vendors. It should be said, RFIs are more common in the government purchasing landscape. The process is a bit too arduous for regular businesses.

Whether or not there's an RFI, the next step is to create the actual request for proposal (RFP) document which will be used to solicit bids from vendors. The RFP document is typically around

100+ pages, and eighty of those pages are full of compliance-related "check the box" information (e.g., "there must be X number of contractors"). However, there are so many different things that get stuck into an RFP that much of it just gets lost in the shuffle.

When the RFP is published, there is a period of time in which bidders review the solicitation and have the opportunity to ask, and a vast sea of vendors can now respond with their bids. Vendors sometimes have entire teams who do nothing but respond to RFPs day in and day out, and they might have multiple teams for various segments of the business: one team responding to B2B requests, another responding to B2G requests, and so on.

Let's be frank. Vendors hate reading and responding to RFPs. Often, they're written by people who don't know the ins and outs of the particular technology they're looking for or written by the incumbent. But why would they? When you're the CIO of a company, you might read industry rags, go to events, and talk about different technologies with vendors, but it's incredibly hard to be an expert at something when you're pulled in many different directions. This is going to be reflected in the RFPs you publish. Nevertheless, vendors want to sell their products and services, so they read and respond to them anyway.

On the other hand, I know of vendors who absolutely refuse to play the RFP game. Some of them are fantastic at what they do but they don't even allow themselves a seat at the table because RFP's are such a drag on internal resources. Those vendors would rather spend their sales and business development efforts elsewhere for better outcomes. With such small win percentages with RFPs, they figure the juice is not worth the squeeze. Their lack of participation in the RFP process means there are some highly skilled, highly successful vendors that the company issuing the RFP will never now about. That's a shame.

Up to this point, the whole RFP process has been as slow as molasses, but once vendor responses start flowing in, the process achieves a snail's pace as the company starts going through the many, many responses. Bear in mind, vendors are going to push solutions that line up with what's best for their own companies. They want to sell their solutions, whether or not those solutions are right for the project, company, or even the industry.

Unfortunately, the company that put out the RFP now has to wade through all of these vendors responses to identify a subset of them that seem appropriate. That subset of vendors will then be interviewed individually in another long, drawn-out process in order to winnow down the list of vendors further.

We could dive even deeper into this part of the process, but you get the picture. Indeed, you've been through this process many times yourself, so you probably already know from hard experience that the average RFP process takes nine to twelve months from start to finish. Sadly, that often means a six-to-twelve-month process that ultimately get you to a solution that might not 100 percent meet your need, or that you quickly outgrow before you're ready (or able) to pay for another upgrade. It happens, we see it more than you would think.

Dealing with Chicken Little

So, why do companies insist on going through this process? In some cases, it seems like they could almost skip every step entirely and just hire a vendor based on a recommendation. Are they going through it just to go through it?

Sometimes, it seems like they go through it just to say they did, or it's a company policy to get a certain number of bids. Perhaps it makes a large tech investment feel more justified when you've used the "tried and true" method for selecting a solution. Even so, the question must be asked, "Why hasn't a more streamlined version of the RFP process already been developed and adopted in every industry?"

A big reason is that change is a pain. People resist change

sometimes, even when it's for the best, because it's not easy, and they're used to doing it the old way. Thus, when you try to implement some sweeping change to an ingrained process, even if that process is clunky and wastes time, you get a bit of a Chicken Little response from some of your people: "The sky is falling! The sky is falling!"

You've no doubt experienced this is many ways, not just related to RFPs. Some people will moan and complain about any change at all, even when it is clearly in the best interests of every single person in the company. In fact, from personal experience, I've *never* seen a transition to a new process that didn't have at least a few Chicken Little-types complaining about it. There's comfort in routine, even when that routine is extremely inefficient, because people know what they're doing. They don't have to learn anything new, so they can fall back on rote behavior. For some companies, the people managing the RFP/procurement process might want these long projects as a matter of job security.

But imagine a brand-new RFP process that 1) engages all stakeholders so you know you've identified the need clearly, 2) is streamlined so it gets you to the right vendors much, much faster, and 3) minimizes the Chicken Little response from your people. That's what our new and better approach to requests for proposal does. Yes, it's possible to stave off the transition jitters, while also getting everyone involved in the change.

But maybe you're not yet sold completely on the *need* for a radically new approach to RFPs, so let me make it crystal clear just how behind the times the current process really is.

CHAPTER TWO

SUPERSONIC SPEED OF CHANGE

"Technological change is not additive; it is
ecological. A new technology does not merely
add something; it changes everything"."

— Neil Postman

Technology changes not just from generation to generation, or from decade to decade, but from year to year. What is considered cutting edge today will be routine tomorrow, and it will probably be obsolete the day after that.

Indeed, we're seeing things moving so fast now that it has made purchasing new tech a more daunting prospect than ever before. I can't count the number of times I've seen a client buy some new platform or tech without being able to account for their next three years of tech growth and development, only to run out of bandwidth, processing power, or storage before their contract is up.

I've also seen people invest in building their own platforms, only to find that the platform no longer meets their needs after years of development. Things are changing so fast that scalability has become an extreme challenge. It's almost impossible to scale if you don't know what's going to happen in the future.

Look at the challenge of data storage. How much storage are you going to need in three years? If you underestimate, you could find yourself in a real bind when your need outpaces your expectations. This is constant problem! Our tech needs grow exponentially every two or three years. How in the world can we possibly keep up?

If you're old enough, you remember how it was when companies just used file cabinets to store their "data." Those file cabinets took up a certain amount of space somewhere in your office, but they were concrete objects. You could see and estimate the amount of space you needed to store paper files. Additionally, if you had compliance requirements, you had to keep those files for a certain number of years, and you knew how long it was before you could toss them out and free up some space.

Now, it's all just data, massive amounts of data, which require massive amounts of storage on Amazon Web Services or somewhere comparable. AWS, Azure or Google are $20 to $30 per terabyte, or whatever the cost happens to be, and you keep pumping the data in, like a firehose that never shuts off. It just grows and grows without end. Data and more data pours into your business every day, and the rate of growth is out of control. The good news is, data storage on a PC or server is significantly cheaper than the square footage needed for file cabinets.

Talk to Me Now

And data storage is just one area of technology that is growing at a rate that is almost impossible to keep up with. Think about all of the ways we communicate now in the business world. At one time, your only real communications technology was the telephone, and you couldn't call someone if they weren't physically present.

Now, there are a dozen different ways to communicate with people, from text and messaging services, to phone services, social media, and various apps, and since your smartphone ostensibly goes wherever you go, younger generations expect to be able to get hold of anyone at any time.

"I texted him, and he hasn't responded for two minutes! What's wrong with him? Is he ignoring me, or did something bad happen to him?" That's the way people think these days. They feel this way about friends and family, but the same attitude applies when they have to interact with a business.

Even as a fifty-one-year-old man, I find it unacceptable to sit on hold waiting to talk to a customer service rep. That stated, I've not so patiently waited through the cheesy on hold music and listened to the 29th time you hear, "Your call is important to us, someone will be with you in just a moment." Increasingly, people expect and demand instant communication access. If a company can't respond and solve their problem in five minutes, the consumer is going to give a negative review. Furthermore, they expect to be able to communicate with a business using their own preferred form of communication. The generation that has had a $1,000 cell phone in their hands since fifth grade and expects immediate gratification has tremendous purchasing power—and that has shifted the way business is done.

This has brought tremendous change especially to the ways businesses connect to their customers such as contact centers. Think about how simple it used to be: If a customer had a problem, they either wrote a letter and waited for a response to show up in their mailbox, or they called the company's 800 number and waited to talk to a representative directly. If it was busy or the holiday season, you waited because there wasn't another way.

Now, companies are also expected to have chat (or, at least, chatbots), text messaging, email, forums, an active social media presence on multiple platforms, and a dedicated app. Omnichannel customer service has become vital because you have to meet your customers where *and how* they want to be met. Otherwise, they'll find someone else who will.

Think about it. When the average twenty-year-old guy wants to order a sub sandwich from the local deli, he's probably not going to call in his order. Instead, he's going to try to text it or choose it from an app or website: "I want a turkey sub with American cheese, tomatoes, and lettuce." And then he's going to expect that sub sandwich to be delivered to his doorstep within a few minutes.

If the deli is run by some old-school business leader who can't or won't meet these expectations, they're going to drive away a lot of young customers, who will think, "Wait a minute! You expect me to walk *into* the store and order the sandwich *at* the deli counter from an actual person and then stand there waiting for it to be made? No thanks! I have a life to live."

There's No Escaping Evolution

The world is changing. There's no escaping it. If you don't make well-informed decisions about your tech, with a clear sense of what the future might hold, you will suffer unanticipated negative consequences.

At one time, data security was easier. Now, it's big business because the bad guys have figured out how to make a lot of money capturing your data with ransomware attacks or disrupting services with DDoS attacks that use multiple machines to bury your server. Then they can contact you and say, "Pay us X amount of Bitcoin, and we'll release your data and stop the attack."

When I was starting out in business, this kind of attack wasn't even in the realm of possibility. Even now, many companies are underprepared for such an attack because they don't realize just how devious and insidious the hackers and data thieves are becoming.

We've gotten to the point where entire businesses are run on servers, so if the server goes down, the whole business is put on hold. Yet I see some companies making ill-advised cost-cutting decisions about their technology services and paying the price for it. The irony is that you didn't buy the service because you thought it cost too much but, when negatively impacted, you would pay 5 or 10 times as much to not be in that pickle. It's like wanting to buy flood insurance after your home has flooded.

Recently, we had a big telecommunications outage in our area, and it put one of our clients, a doctor's practice, in a bind. The practice had two locations: a main office and a satellite office. At the main office, we had installed SD WAN, which intelligently routes traffic over multiple circuits so when the one ISP failed, the network remained up. This ensures that there's always connectivity, so when the network went out, their traffic was routed to another circuit. They never missed a beat.

However, their satellite office was much smaller. I recommended that they put an additional connection with SD WAN there as well, but they didn't think it was necessary. Consequently, the outage negatively impacted them. Suddenly, all of the connected services at their satellite location went down, which meant, among other things, that they couldn't access patient medical records in the office. They were forced to send patients home because they simply couldn't treat them without access to their records. The revenue lost on that one day would have paid for the redundant connection for the year, if not more.

The next day, they called us and asked us to install another connection to their satellite location. I don't blame them for being unprepared for the outage. It's hard to keep up with the rate of change and how it impacts your tech needs. At one time, having a primary connection to your data network was enough, and if you had a backup connection, it was an added bonus in case of a very rare problem. However, if your network went down, it didn't bring business to a standstill. The backup was merely an insurance policy. Chances are all the files you needed to access were stored locally on your network.

Indeed, many companies choose to use both connections at the same time because they need to consume such a vast quantity of data and all their applications live in the cloud. So, they push traffic over both connections and simply prioritize traffic as needed. For example, voice and video usually gets prioritized to ensure its stability. That's why SD-WAN is rapidly becoming the network standard. The money spent on a second circuit is no longer an insurance policy, it's a necessary cost of doing business.

Then there's wireless service. In 1996, if you wanted wireless phone service, you could lug around a brick with a huge antenna. Now, most people carry around cell phones that are vastly more powerful than the computers that put men on the moon. Getting a cell phone when you're about eight years old is practically a rite of passage these days, just like getting a car at sixteen. We've all seen it: Pre-teens walk around with thousand-dollar iPhones, and scarcely anyone bats an eye.

And customers of all ages expect to be able to interact with any type of business in any way they want to through their cellphone. That means a website that is fully mobile friendly, a dedicated app, and an active presence on whatever the popular social media platforms of the day happen to be. For some businesses, it can be hard to keep up with. "We're supposed to be active where, on what app, in what way?"

The Evolution of Technology

LETS TAKE A LOOK AT HOW JUST A FEW MAJOR CATAGORIES OF TECHNOLOGY HAVE CHANGED IN RECENT DECADES. THIS BY NO MEANS AN EXHAUSTIVE LIST, BUT EVEN A CURSORY OVERVIEW CAN BE BREATHTAKING.

THE INTERNET

1969

ARPANET launches, which is the blueprint of what will eventually become the internet.

1972

ARPANET is officially swiched to TCP/IP

1998

Google is founded. innovating the business of point and click.

2006

Amazon Web Services begins marketing IT infrastructure to businesses. and the term "cloud computing" gains traction.

2009

The creation of the Bitcoin network, which made this the first blockchain to securely execute verifiable transactions without needing central authorities.

2022

Building on the growth of blockchain protocols, advanced decentralized networks have the potential to foster new, user-oriented service models that can replace surveillance capitalism and create a more resilient and secure internet that redirects value and control to the public.

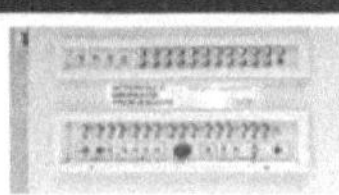

1972

Email, the internet's first killer app, is integrated into the ARPANET networks File Transfer Protocol.

1990

Tim Berners-Lee develops prototype for the WORLD WIDE WEB.

1995

Amazon, Yahoo, and eBay launch, signaling the beginning of consumerism on the web

2004

Facebook was created. signaling a new era of social media on the internet.

2007

Biggest innovation of this year was the iPhone, which renewed interest in mobile web applications.

2014

Google enforced HTTPS encryption by default for safer internet browsing and connncetion.

2019

5G Technology started rolling out in 5G-ready areas

Data Centers

Data center trace their roots back to the 1940's, when the Electronic Numerical Integrator and Computer ((ENIAC) was the pinnacle of the computational technology.

1950's

U.S Harry Truman had ENIAC center built at military installations. He assigned engineers and researchers from the, newly formed CIA, to assist in the development and innovation of ENIAC technology at the dawn of the Cold War.

Early data centers were incredibly complex. Their primary purpose was geared towards intelligence and military functions; therefore, secrecy was important. Huge vents and fans were needed for cooling hundreds of feet of wiring and vacuum tubes to connect all the components were also needed. Wires often overheated and failed

1960 -1970s

Computational technology skyrocketed. In the early 60's, IBM released their first transistorized computer called TRADIC. This new model eliminated vacuum tubes systems, which allowed data center to be used by commercial entities as well. Computer systems could now be fit into multipurpose spaces like office buildings.

Through the 60's and 70's, companies like IBM, Intel Xerox, and Sun Microsystems heralded the arrival of the personal computer in the 80's.

Between the 80's and 90, users began to interface with servers located in data centers around the world using the newly-developed Internet, laying the ground work for the modern data center.

2019

According to the 2019 Annual CyberCrime Report, the world will lose $6 billion to Cyber Crime in 2021, up from $3 billion the year before.

IBM has added a new member to its Spectrum Scale Enterprise Storage Server (ESS)

2022

IBM launches a software-defined storage server fot AI.

DATA STORAGE

1804

An innovative Frenchman Joseph-Marie Jacquard patented his invention of cards with punched holes which held weaving instructions for the Jacquard Loom. Punched cards automated the process, allowing even unskilled workers to efficiently manufacture intricate patterns.

1928

Magnetic Tape Drive held about 230KB of data.

1833: Charles Babbage constructs the first punched card machine with a memory store called the Analytical Engine.

1932

Magnetic drums, invented by Gustav Tauschek which only had 48KB of storage.

A Magnetic Drum
This magnetic drum added additional storage to the Whirlwind computer in the early 1950s. (Image courtesy of The MITRE Corporation Archives.)

1947

The first form of RAM was invented by Williamns-Kilburn, it only help 1258 bytes of storage.

1951

Magnetic Core was the first cores stored little more than 2KB called the Magnetic Core .

1956

The first hard disk drive introduced by IBM. it weighted over a ton and was the size of a refrigerator. The first HHDs could hold 3.75MB

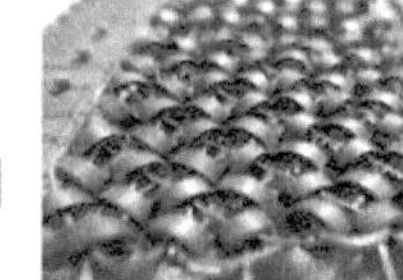

1951: Jay Forrester files a patent application for the matrix core memory

1982

The Compact Disk (CD) was developed by both Sony and Philips which had the capacity of 650-700MB.

November 1996, Toshiba introduced the world's first DVD player, the SD-3000, as a result of developments initiated in 1994.

1995

Digital Video (DVD) was also developed by Sony and Philips. the first DVD had 1.46 GB of storage

Cyber Security

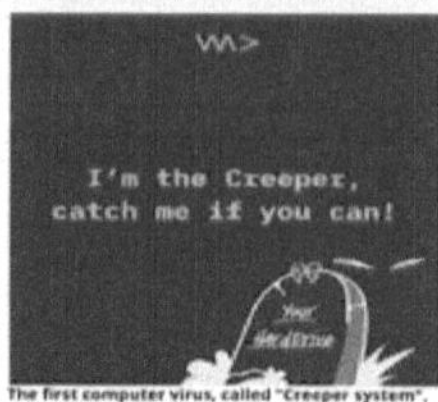

The first computer virus, called "Creeper system", was an experimental self-replicating virus released in 1971

1971

The Creeper and Reaper: Regarded as the worlds's first virus, it was not meant to be malicious. It would print a message saying "I'm the creeper: catch me if you can!".

1988

The Norris Worm: A worm code that was meant to gauge the size of the internet, it replicated incessantly, which clogged Arpanet and caused 10% of systems to crash

2003

The Birth of Anonymous: The most popular hacktivist group. Anonymous is decentralized international hacktivist collective which carries out cyber attacks in order

From 2008 - 2012, Anonymous managed to execute many hacks, with effects that ranged from inconsequential to critical.

2009

Operation Aurora: A series of cyber attacks that originated in China targeting more than thirty U.S private-sector companies such as Google, Yahoo, and Adobe.

2010

Stuxnet: An extremely sophisticated computer worm that exploited multiple Windows vulnerabilities.

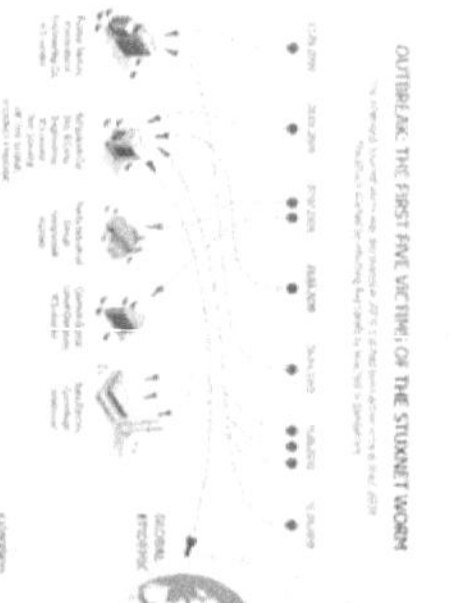

2017

Eternal Blue and Ransomware Attacks: An exploit that utilized vulnerabilities in the Windows implementation of the Server Message Block protocol. It was leaked WannaCry and NotPetya

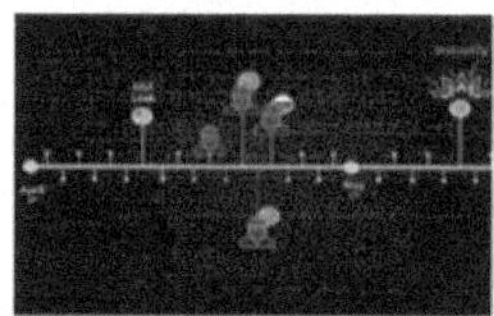

2019

According to the 2019 Annual CyberCrime Report, the world will lose $6 billion to Cyber Crime in 2021, up from $3 billion the year before.

2020

The Twitter Hack: The accounts of numerous high profile twitter users were hacked. The hackers tried to get people to send them bitcoin by posing as the high profile celebrities. They made 86,000 pounds within a few hours .

I share all of these examples to confirm one singular point (and problem): that almost every area of technology has changed—and continues to change—in astonishing ways, and it's all happening so fast that people are struggling to anticipate and keep up with the changes.

But then there are RFPs. Requests for proposal haven't change one single bit. Think about it. Has anything—anything at all—changed about the RFP process? Has anything gotten faster, better, more efficient, or more effective? Admittedly, there might be some online tools that organize things better than the old stacks of paper, but the core internal process and external vendor engagement remain unchanged. If you went through the RFP process thirty or forty years ago, you would have followed the same basic steps.

And here's where the pace of technological evolution becomes a problem. First, if you can't keep up with what you need as a company both now and in the future, then it becomes harder to craft an RFP that will get you where you truly need to go. Second, the rate of change in technology requires the people writing RFPs to really be up-to-date on current tech. Otherwise, you might end up writing an RFP for tech that will be obsolete in a year or two years.

Indeed, I've seen people write RFPs that were completely misguided. I know of a company that wrote an RFP for some incredibly outdated technology because they didn't understand how much the industry had changed. They were just trying to get a better price on technology they already knew, but they wound up making a really expensive decision on tech that was obsolete the moment they installed it. When the RFP hit my desk, I thought it was about as effective as doing an RFP for an 8-track tape player.

I've seen other companies buy decent tech that was great when they installed it, but it failed to match their rate of growth and became a roadblock to their company's success two or three years down the road. When that happens, companies often find themselves having to invest in another expensive solution long before they've realized the ROI on the initial purchase.

This happens far too often, and it can be a massive headache. A customer of mine told me one such story. They went through an RFP process and wound up investing in a network solution that they thought would be big enough for their future growth. They had a headquarters site (their hub site) and thirty or forty smaller locations, and all of the traffic from the smaller sites was funneled through the hub.

Unfortunately, though they had made estimates during the early stages of their RFP process, they had misjudged just how much traffic would be flowing through their headquarters site. It turned out to be a lot more than they anticipated, and they soon pegged the HQ circuit which made the overall performance of their network terrible. Calls were getting dropped left and right, and they were losing customers—all because traffic was burying the hub circuit.

Finally, they came to us for help, and we had to inform the that it would take sixty days to upgrade their circuit. That meant limping along for just a little but longer. Unfortunately, upgrading also required a significant financial investment from them, even though they'd already made a significant investment on the initial network installation a couple of years earlier.

And that's just *one* problem with RFPs. The more pervasive problem is just the sheer amount of time that you have to spend trying to find a single solution. It's hard enough trying to keep up with all of the changes, but every time you decide to upgrade, you face the prospect of another six-to-twelve-month RFP process to get to a solution. And, of course, many of the vendor responses you get aren't even going to meet your needs.

There's always a negative "aha" moment that happens when you're an hour into reading a hundred-page RFP and realize, "These guys can't do what I'm asking. Their solution is all wrong." So, you set that response side and pick up the next one. Over and over again, hour after hour. And even after all of that, even after reading every response and interviewing dozens of vendors, there's no guarantee you'll wind up with the right solution or a solution that can keep pace with your growth.

At Your Wit's End

I spoke to a business owner recently who was incredibly frustrated because he'd been shopping for a service that could meet some specific needs at a very affordable price. By the time he spoke to us, he'd already had five failed deployments after going through countless responses to his RFP, and none of them could really do what he wanted.

All combined, the poor guy and his team had spent hundreds of hours trying to figure out exactly what they needed, pushing it out to vendors, and then wading through responses and interviewing vendors just trying to find someone—anyone—who could do what they wanted at a price they could afford. He had deployed or partially deployed solutions only to find out the vendors were missing key components of what he needed.

By the time I talked to him, he was a year into his RFP process, and he was at his wit's end. And I told him what I've told many frustrated people who have been worn down by the RFP process. In my eyes there were three problems he was facing : 1) he hadn't clearly defined his present and future wants/needs, 2) he was putting too much emphasis on price first, and 3) he had absolutely no idea how to manage the whole process because it wasn't his day job.

Fortunately, I was also able to show this poor frustrated soul that there is indeed a better way, and when I walked him through our RFP Alternative process, he was amazed. He said, "Wait a minute. We can do this differently? I had no idea there was another option for RFPs." He had become an unwanted expert at that technology solution at the expense of growing his new company. Where could his company be if he had the right partner from the beginning?

It's something I've heard a lot. Companies simply don't know there are options. They spend countless hours narrowing down a list of vendors just so those vendors can send their sales rep to tell them, "Here's why we're the best thing in the world." And in the end, they have to sort through so much information and so many claims to make a purchasing decision that is based on what they *thought* they needed without any real certainty if it will continue to meet their needs long enough to justify the investment.

In another instance, I spoke to a company that had gone through an RFP process three years earlier to buy a phone system. After many months, they wound up buying a solution from a LSV (Large Sucky Vendor). A smart and persistent LSV sales rep managed to sell this company a system for $60,000 that they did not really need, and when the company realized this, it was too late. They were locked into a contract for three years that they could not get out of.

Worse yet, they learned later on that if they decided to switch vendors, they had to pay to upgrade the system to go to the other vendor. The cost was astronomical. The dictionary definition of mad as hell is the moment the business owner realizes that he now has $60,000 worth of phones that should have lasted 10-12 years that are worth maybe $2800 on the gray market after three years.

These kinds of situations happen all too often with tech upgrades. You can apply it to any kind of hardware. People make purchases that pigeonhole them into spending a lot of money for a solution that either does not really meet their needs or that they soon outgrow—all because a vendor sales rep guides them to specific solution for the wrong reason.

Sometimes, the purchase makes total sense at the time, but then the vendor gets acquired a year later, and suddenly the service level goes to hell in a handbasket. I've seen that more than once.

That is the purchasing paradox. You settle on a vendor after a long and frustrating search and jump in the deep end of the pool with them, but the solution doesn't end up working out. In the end, it costs you a fortune to fix the problem and it is all on you to drive the outcomes.

It almost seems like an impossible situation, doesn't it? You can't possibly acquire all of the knowledge you need about the rate of technological change, your own growth in coming years, relevant industry trends, *and* specific vendors. Now multiply that by all the different technology solutions you have within your business, and you are buried in the quicksand of analysis paralysis. So, you end up wading through dozens of RFP responses and talking to vendors who only try to sell their own company's solution, whether it's a good fit or not.

And what makes this situation even worse is that the purchasing landscape had changed. It's harder to find that right solution to meet your specific need than ever before, especially if you want a solution that you're not going to outgrow too quickly. Next, let's take a look at how purchasing is getting even more difficult.

CHAPTER THREE

THE EVOLVING PURCHASING LANDSCAPE

"If the buyer walks off the lot, our chances of getting them back into the dealership are slim to none—and slim left town."

—Tim Kintz

Think about how the process of buying a car has changed. You used to rely on a car salesperson to take you through the journey. The salesperson would walk you physically onto the car lot, open a car, and let you get inside. You'd smell the new car smell, check out the flashy interior, rub your hands across the soft leather seats, and then they would hand you the key so you could go for a ride. If you liked it, you'd go back into the sales office and haggle over the price.

During that process, as you tried to talk the salesperson down to a lower price, they would occasionally mutter, "I'll see what I can do," and walk out of the room to discuss the price with a sales manager. They would usually come back with a counter-offer, and the haggling would continue. Eventually, you'd both agree to a price. You'd make the purchase, and you'd all celebrate the moment.

I remember a friend of mine, many years ago went to the local dealership to buy a car, and he took a suitcase with him that contained exactly $9,999 in cash. The asking price for the vehicle was about $11 or $12k so, he approached the salesman and said, "Go and tell your sales manager I'll buy it with this cash right here right now."

So, the salesman walked out of the room for few minutes, and as he walked back over to us, he said, "My sales manager says we can do $10,500."

My friend picked up the suitcase and promptly walked out of the dealership. The salesman and the manager chased him into the parking lot, shouting, "Okay, we'll take the deal! We'll take it! Don't leave!"

That kind of direct interaction and haggling was the old way of making a purchase. Nowadays, by the time a customer walks into a car dealership, they have already used an internet rep to negotiate prices, and they know exactly what they want and exactly what it's worth. They might print all of this information, or at least save it on their phone, and they'll take it with them into the dealership.

"This is what I want right now," they'll say, showing the salesperson the information, "and this is what I'll pay for it. The internet says the car is worth this much. And this will be my monthly payment

In other words, people these days have generally done their homework before they make a purchase. The internet has made the end user much more informed than they used to be about everything, including technology.

Unfortunately, at the same time, there is a whole lot more noise out there. There's just so much information, and so many different claims, that it can be hard to wade through it all. This becomes a problem when you're trying to find the best solution to a specific problem. Even when you try to do your due diligence and find information about available solutions, the sheer volume of information and various vendor claims can actually obscure the truth.

Additionally, some people don't realize that not all tech services are the same. They assume one VoIP service is the same as another. One cloud storage service is the same as another. One SD WAN solution is the same as another. They think the only real difference is the price because some companies charge more than others. And, of course, this is simply not the case. There are many unique features, functionalities, integrations, and variables that make some solutions more suitable for a specific customer than others. Just because you need voice over internet protocol does not mean any company's VoIP solution will be right for you.

But how can you figure out which one is best? It's not easy to track down this information when you don't know where to look. Every company that provides VoIP is going to claim that their service will perfectly meet your needs because they want to make a sale. However, validating a salesperson's claims through online research can quickly become an exercise in frustration.

All of this makes it easier for people to make a bad buying decision, even after months and months of exhaustive work. By the time they realize they bought a suboptimal solution, it's too late to undo it.

The Source of Buyer's Remorse

I'm not intentionally picking on Cisco but using this as an example of how the same services can actually be slightly different and why that matters. Cisco Meraki MX is a multifunctional SD-WAN (software-defined wide-area network), a product that uses software to control multiple data connections between company headquarters, data centers and remote branches or applications. It's a great product that will fit most SD WAN needs. However, when the Meraki solution kicks over to a new ISP circuit to manage traffic, it drops the current session.

That means, for example, if you're a medical practice and you've got someone parked on the phone and validating appointments, when the connection switches to a new circuit, it will drop the call with the customer. Of course, that's not a good thing. It's never a good idea to drop calls on the people who are paying your bills.

Other SD-WAN products from other companies will push packets to both circuits, which guarantees that they go through. That means, even if a packet drops, you never lose the call. That's a pretty big difference between products offering the same solution, one which could directly impact your business, so it matters which SD-WAN product you choose.

For another example, we can look at Amazon Web Services and Azure, both of which provide cloud storage services. Both are fairly cheap, and they seem like the greatest thing ever, right? You can dump a ton of data there for a little bit of money. There's just one problem. If you ever need to get that data back, you have to pay a little something called "egress fees."

Egress fees will cost you an arm and a leg, but they're rarely talked about and not usually mentioned up front. You will find details about egress fees buried in the small print on page forty-seven of a website you don't know about. You also can't do anything about them. If you want your data back, you have to pay them. It can be quite a shock when you need to grab your data for a system upgrade and suddenly discover that it'll cost you $20,000. Now, you're stuck, but you've uploaded so much data that you can't even put it anywhere else.

This is a huge source of buyer's remorse with cloud storage services. If your business has to transfer data regularly, whether for compliance or some other reason, then you probably don't want to use AWS or Azure. You're better off going somewhere with low or no egress fees, even if you have to pay a little more for each terabyte of storage. Many people just don't know this. They think all cloud storage services are essentially the same.

Vendors don't generally tell you about hidden fees, administrative costs, and penalties during the bidding process. It's buried in the fine print. Unless you comb through the fine print, you'll have to learn the hard way that what you budgeted at $500 actually winds up costing you $800. Sometimes, these hidden fees are mandated by the federal government. Other times, they are just costs added by the company because they can.

Also, there are auto-renewal clauses in most technology contracts that kick in unless you notify them that you do not intend to renew within ninety days of the end of your contract. If you reach out on day eighty-nine, they'll say, "Sorry, too late. You missed your window." And suddenly, you're locked in for another three years. Auto-renewals are just funny money as well because the vendor is not on the hook to their underlying vendors for the added three years. At month 72 of the relationship with that vendor, you are now paying prices that were negotiated 6 years earlier in an industry where costs often are reduced at renewal time.

The point is, all services aren't the same, and there are a lot of variables that can make the wrong version of the right service a very bad choice for you. Buyer's remorse is rampant, and it can be particularly frustrating after a long, agonizing RFP process to discover this the hard way.

Similarly, just because there's some sexy new technology out there doesn't mean it makes sense for every customer. In another case, I had a customer who was using older data technology. It worked just fine for them, but there was newer technology on the market that looked amazing. However, their application used very short data packets, so they had no need for the big bandwidth provided by the new tech. Even though it was supposed to be the latest and greatest thing, they would have wound up paying a lot more for bandwidth that they didn't need.

Fortunately, I was able to point this out to them, because a vendor for the newer tech might not have said it. Any information they found online would have confused the issue. It would have been very easy for them to make an unwise purchasing decision if we hadn't done an evaluation and explained the situation.

The Importance of a Technology Specialist

Instead of following the herd, doing what everyone else is doing, listening to the first vendor who comes along, or getting confused by all the noise from all of the different sources online, it's important to approach your own needs like you have a blank slate. This is the approach we always like to use. We get a whiteboard and ask the client, "Tell us everything that is important to *you*." In other words, begin by *very clearly* determining what you need and what you want.

I know of a certain company that put in a bid on a cheap phone system and only realized after the fact that their inexpensive solution didn't have enough programmable buttons to create park features, which they desperately needed. They wound up having to deploy an all-new solution. Park buttons were a HUGE part of their day to day business, but they made the mistake of assuming all systems were the same. In this case they were not.

I don't blame any of the companies I've mentioned in this chapter for making suboptimal purchasing decisions. And I don't necessarily blame vendors either. A vendor's job is to champion their company's products, not police a potential customer's purchasing decisions. Still, you don't know what you don't know, and you don't often have a vendor-neutral, educated advisor to walk you through the process of defining your own needs and finding the right solution. Know-how and experience matters.

I made the mistake once years ago of firing my accountant and trying to do payroll taxes by myself. Did I ever screw up and it wound up costing me very dearly because I didn't know what the hell I was doing! It was a painful lesson learned. You have to have someone who knows the environment. Fortunately, I learned that from the accountant experience. Now, I find people who can speak through the noise. When my company looked for a CRM system, I hired a CRM specialist, and it was game-changing.

Even though I paid the specialist thousands for her advice, she was able to find the exact right solution and customize it to our specific needs. She was able to talk to me at my level and craft a solution that was exactly what we wanted. I never would have been able to do it on my own in a million years, even with tons of information online. Most so-called specialists would have pointed me to a specific product whether it was right or not. And in the end, the solution we wound up with might have cost us far more than what I paid in terms of frustration, corrections, and workarounds.

Human nature tends to try to buy things on the cheap. I'm guilty of this myself at times. However, things are getting so much more complex, and technology is evolving so quickly, that it pays to get the right advice: vendor neutral and highly educated. Specialization matters more than ever.

You need a specialist who can help you identify exactly what you need and what will work best for your business based on your skill set, resources, and the platforms you have access to. What if, instead of trying to navigate the complexity of the tech world to make a purchasing decision on your own, you had a specialist who was totally committed to your success, someone who could show you more in twenty minutes than you could figure out on your own through Google searches in six to nine months?

There's a classic story about specialization. A company had been having problems with their equipment. The assembly line kept stopping and interrupting production, and they weren't sure why. It was costing them a fortune in lost revenues. They'd tried to solve the problem on their own by doing their own research. When that proved to be too challenging, they hired an expert who charged them $20,000. He came into their factory, examined their equipment for a few minutes, then turned a single knob. And that was it. The problem was solved with the single turn of a knob, and it cost the company $20,000.

The business leader complained, but the expert replied, "You didn't pay me $20,000 to turn a knob. You paid $20,000 for the knowledge I possess, which told me that turning a knob would solve your problem—something you could not have figured out on your own."

Indeed, despite the cost, he'd saved them a whole lot of frustration, *and* he saved them a lot of lost revenue from production problems over the long run. Getting the right information is invaluable, and if it leads to the right solution, then it's always a smart investment. Because there's another big problem that makes it hard to find to the right solution for your need.

Yes, the rate of change is fast and furious, and it can be hard to keep up. Yes, the purchasing landscape makes the process of selecting the best solution more difficult. But there's another issue: We are being bombarded constantly by voices telling us to, "Buy this. Buy that." Somehow, we must quiet the noise to hear what we *need* to hear.

CHAPTER FOUR

QUIET THE NOISE

"Of the varieties of modern pollution,
noise is the most insidious."
— Robert Lacey

Maybe you remember the old Verizon Wireless commercials where a man in glasses holds a cell phone to his ear while walking around, saying, "Can you hear me now?" That man had a name, "Test Man," and the gimmick of the ad campaign was to place him in unusual locations: on a topical beach, in a desert, on a rowboat in the middle of the Hudson, in a wheat field, and so on.

It's been quite a few years since that ad campaign ran, but it seems like an appropriate metaphor for the sheer amount of marketing noise that bombards us these days. Except, instead of one man walking around saying it, we have thousands of people shouting it at us constantly: "Can you hear me now?"

We face a steady stream of commercials, spam emails, direct mail, Linked In messages, and uninvited sales pitches: "Buy this! Buy that!" The situation is particularly bad for IT leaders, who are bombarded with phone calls from salespeople constantly trying to sell them things. Indeed, I had an IT manager contact me recently, and the first thing he said was, "My phone rings off the hook all day long. You have to help me!"

Maybe you've had a similar experience. Maybe this is your experience *right now.* You're inundated with people promoting an endless variety of solutions. No wonder things get murky when you have to make a purchasing decision. When you're looking for a tech solution, it's like asking a question in a crowded room and getting a hundred different answers at the same time. How are you supposed to hear the right answer through all of those voices speaking over each other?

When I think of this, I can't help but think about a time when I was looking to refinance my house. I went on Lending Tree and put my information and clicked send. Holy Crap!!! I did not so much as take a breath when my phone started ringing. They called day and night, over and over again. It was relentless! Note cards in the mail, e mails, planes flying banners overhead with mortgage rates like you see at the beach during the summer. I think I even saw one lender halfway up a tree with binoculars staring into my office waiting for me to come out from under my desk. Maybe I'm exaggerating slightly, but I can't help but think that is the typical day in the life of IT leadership for many companies across the nation.

When that IT manager asked me if I could stop the voices, I had to tell him the truth. "I can't make them stop, but I can make it so you don't have to deal with them anymore. You'll have someone in your corner with access to all of the resources you need, so you can get where you want to go."

You see, even if you can't silence all of the voices, you can at least quiet the noise. How did I achieve it for this individual? By helping him to clarify his destination and giving him an answer to the endless litany of sales pitches. Now, he could say to those salespeople, "I work with a technology broker, and he knows my wants, needs, and has access to incredible resources. I don't need what you're trying to sell."

And not only so, but he no longer had to tell and re-tell his story every time he wanted to look into some new technology. I could be his voice in a sense, wading through the sea of noise to get him to the right destination. By learning about his business, whiteboarding his wants and needs, I could guide him through that room full of shouting voices to the correct answer.

My head is always on a swivel, bringing vetted solutions to the people I work with, knowing what their needs are. Sometimes, their answer to a recommended solution is *no* (or *not now*), but at least they are now equipped with knowledge about a service specific to their needs. Often, I bring things to them that they didn't even know existed.

Don't Take a Leap of Faith

It's a nice feeling when you can cut through all the claims to find a customer a very specific solution that makes sense for them financially and addresses their needs perfectly. Recently, we were able to find and recommend a certain SMS text messaging platform to a retail customer. You might wonder why a retail customer would need a texting platform. As it turned out, they wanted to be able to push out time-sensitive messages to key shoppers at a moment's notice: "Special price just this week."

If they send a text like that to 10,000 customers and get only 1 percent response, it still means a hundred customers came to the store because of that text and made a purchase. That might not seem like much, but what if the average order from those customers was $200? That would mean the store made $20,000 with just a single text using a platform that costs them about $30 to $40 a month. Not a bad deal. It was a niche need, and we were able to cut through a lot of other product sales pitches to find the best solution for them. Now, their phone system isn't just a line-item expense on their P&L, it's a marketing tool that generates revenue for them.

Another client of ours runs a business on the second floor of a building. They have running water in the ceiling above them, and they have servers in a room that is 10 degrees cooler than the depths of hell even with three fans blowing on them. To get to their desks in the back of the room, you have to step over all of the power cords. When we saw this, we realized it was a perfect storm just waiting to happen.

Their entire business was on those servers! When I walked through the room, I said, "You're running a real risk of losing everything here. If you spring a leak upstairs, this will become a disaster site." So, we reviewed disaster recovery as a service solution for them, which meant backing up everything onsite and also into the cloud.

Now, if something goes wrong, they will be able to run their business from the backup. We bid it out to numerous vendors, and they selected the service that made the most sense for the need and their budget. Of course, in a perfect world, they will never need the backup, but it's not a perfect world. Whether using cloud as a backup or the primary source for running the business, the cloud is a very real part of most, if not all, businesses today. That customer lays their head on the pillow knowing they are covered if the unthinkable becomes a reality.

The challenge in all of this is that we're inundated with technology ads offering solutions to all kinds of problems, but it's just not possible for the average consumer to become an expert in all the technology that touches their life and business every day. This makes it incredibly hard to evaluate the claims of the marketers and vendors. Will this SaaS solution really meet your company's needs? Will this piece of hardware really provide reliable service for your customers?

So many promises are just impossible to validate on your own, which is why a lot of companies end up taking a leap of faith when it comes to purchasing a solution. Even after a long and exhaustive RFP process, where they have identified a handful of vendors with what appear to be suitable solutions for their needs, they still reach a point where they have to cross their fingers and say, "I guess this is the one. Gosh, I hope we're not making a bad investment here."

It would be so much easier if they had an advocate in their corner who wasn't pushing any particular solution, someone who could guide them like a coach to what they need and give them clarity on their choices. I know of a company leader who decided to try to build his own CCaaS (Contact Center as a Service) platform, despite having little practical knowledge about what it would take. If he had crossed his fingers and jumped into this project, he would have soon found himself overwhelmed and overpaying.

Fortunately, as his coach, I was able give him clarity about what it would take to build his own solution. "You will need to buy space in a data center. You will need to buy servers. You're going to have to buy all of the networking equipment across multiple geographical data center locations. And you will need to plan ahead for five years of growth. All of this is going to cost you a ton up front, not to mention all of the time it will take to figure out how to do it on your own."

"Instead," I explained, "if you went with an on-demand cloud-based solution, you would find it much easier to scale. It would be far easier and more cost effective." In the end, this advice saved the company from a huge and expensive headache and put them on the right path. As a new business, it also allowed them to turn a CapEx into a significantly lower OpEx to maintain cash reserves as they grew.

Who Can You Trust?

There are two kinds of decision-makers. Some want to see what they're choosing. They want to walk in the back room and feel the warmth of the servers. They want to touch and hear the buzzing of the hardware. Other folks don't care about a hands-on approach. They just want to know that the technology works. If a button is pushed, the desired outcome is staring them in the face.

No matter which one you are, you need an inner circle of people you can trust to help you make the right decision. There's just too much noise for anyone to be able to wade through these days. Having someone you trust to bounce ideas off of will enable you to cut through the chaos of ads, sales, vendor claims, and information.

As the old saying goes, "Show me who you run with, and I'll show you your future." Do you have someone you trust? Someone you feel comfortable with to sit down and whiteboard your wants and needs? Someone you could approach and say, "Hey, I'm hearing a lot about this new technology. Do you think it would work for us? Could we proof of concept this?"

You need trusted technology advisors to help you wade through the mess, someone without any vendor ties. Better still is a trusted technology advisor who has ties to all of them. After all, if you align yourself with a specific vendor, then they're only going to recommend their own solutions, whether they're right for you or not. A vendor's job is to sell their service. That's the bottom line.

But imagine an advisor who *isn't* trying to sell a specific solution and has no motivation to recommend anything other than what is best for you. They're taking the journey together with you, helping you figure out what is best for you, what's going to drive revenue for your business, boost productivity, and drive stakeholder happiness. Just as you are investing in the trusted technology advisor, they are investing in you as well.

It makes a huge difference. An advisor who is knowingly selling a service versus an advisor who is only interested in helping you find the right solution. Which one would you trust more? I have friends and acquaintances who deal with salespeople all day long trying to convince them to invest in some tech or software solution. These sales reps talk a good game. They'll act like your best friend if they have to, but at the end of the day, it's the transaction that matters most to them—not your needs and wants. They will be long gone by the time you realize there is a problem and someone else is usually on the hook to clean up the mess. Maybe that someone has been you in the past. I'm 100% confident that no sales team in the history of direct sales has ever had a quota of smiley faces, it's always dollars.

That's what a trusted technology advisor does for you. They're committed to your needs, not just to a transaction, and they know that one size does not fit all.

CHAPTER FIVE

ONE SIZE DOES NOT FIT ALL

"Put too many one-size-fits-all jackets on
Americans and the place explodes."
— Lamar Alexander

There's a huge difference between buying a solution "off the rack" and investing in a custom-made solution that has been tailored to your specific needs. It's the difference buying a suit off the rack at Burlington Coat Factory or having it tailored to fit you. The latter option always looks better, fits better, and feels more comfortable because it was made to your unique specifications. Instead of trying to cram your body into a pre-made suit, you're making the suit to the shape of your body.

All technology is not the same, and the real secret sauce in finding the best solution to meet your specific wants and needs is customization. What does this look like in practice? I sat down with a client not long ago to discuss their need for a phone service. We used a whiteboard and started from scratch, discussing what was most important to them and what they wanted. From that, we built out a system that would fit all of their criteria and found vendors who could supply it.

Contrast this with a company that just buys a service "off the shelf" from a vendor who promises them the moon. They need a phone system, so they approach a vendor and ask, "Can your product meet all of our needs?"

"Of course, it can," the direct rep from the vendor replies. "Our phone system is exactly what you need. Now, let's sign the three-year service agreement today!"

And only later, after signing the contract, does the company realize that the product they bought lacks some important functionalities and features that they need. Too late! Now, they're stuck with it for three years.

To be very clear, I'm not accusing all vendors of being shady or lying about the capabilities of their products. On the contrary, I work with many vendors to provide customers with great solutions, and most of them are decent, sincere people who genuinely want to help. However, their job is to believe in, promote, and sell their company's products, not push clients to someone else, so they're not usually going to take a broad view of all the solutions in the marketplace.

A vendor is shooting themselves in the foot if they say, "Our solution would be okay for you, but actually our fiercest competitor offers something closer to what you need." Additionally, a sincere vendor truly believes in the superiority of his company's solution, and this is naturally going to be reflected in the conversation. I'll outline the important differences between vendor direct reps and channel reps a little later in the book because their approach is different.

So, how do you find a customized solution when you're not an expert on all of the services, features, and options that are available out there? The obvious answer is that you bring in an expert who can help you differentiate your needs from the "nice to haves" with a clear understanding of the available solutions and how they fit into your budget.

Of course, figuring out your *real* budget is a challenge in itself.

Think about what 2020 did to a lot of company budgets. Nobody planned to have their entire teams working from home. Suddenly, companies in all kinds of industries had to pay for networking technology and data security at their employee's homes, things they had not budgeted for.

For that reason, when I work with clients, I try to look at their technology spend holistically, recognizing that sometimes your needs may change unexpectedly. When that happens, your budget has to be able to reasonably evolve with your needs, and as an outside expert with a broad and objective view of technology field, I am able to help companies think about it well in advance. We often look at a customer's technology spend holistically, and "robbing Peter to pay Paul" is a very common occurrence with our engagements. We see those projects as a puzzle, trying to fit all the pieces into place to do more with less. It's always a great feeling when you can go into one of your customers and tell them you found a way to pay for the technology that they need but did not think they could afford.

You need a solution that not only meets your specific needs *now*, not only fits within your budget this quarter, but is future-proofed and able to scale with you. It's highly unlikely that some product off the shelf will do all of these things well. Instead of saying, "We need VoIP," you need to be able to say, "We need a VoIP solution customized for our present and future needs."

Finding the Right Technology

Maybe you've used something like Zagat's guide to find a good restaurant when you wanted to dine out. If you have, you know that they give a rating of one to four dollar signs to indicate how expensive a specific restaurant is. Let's suppose you want to go out for Italian food one night so you open the guide and peruse the listings for Italian restaurants in your city.

As it turns out, there are plenty of Italian restaurants to choose from, but they're not all the same, not by a long stretch, even if you see many of the same common Italian dishes on all of their menus. A restaurant with a single dollar sign is going to be a lot cheaper and probably offer a simpler experience, while a four-dollar-sign restaurant is going to be a fine dining experience that will take a big bite out of your wallet. You have to think carefully about what kind of experience you want and need, as well as what your dining budget is for that evening.

We can see the same thing when we look at technology solutions. A "single dollar sign" product or service will offer a bare bones solution that costs the least to deploy and manage. It's a cheap, greasy plate of spaghetti on a paper plate with a Coke at a small hole-in-the-wall place. On the other end of the spectrum, a "four dollar sign" product or service addressing the same problem will offer a solution that is far more expensive but also much faster, more robust, more compliant, and feature rich. It's like a seven-course meal with expensive wine at the very top of the tallest building in town.

You have to decide if you need that fancy meal with many plates of gourmet food or the cheap dinner with greasy pasta on a paper plate. They are not nearly the same, even if they operate in a similar category of cuisine. If you only have the budget for that plate of spaghetti, you're going to be in world of hurt if you turn up at the fine dining restaurant.

"Honey, maybe we don't need to spend $800 on a dinner of white truffle Fiorentina with a $600 bottle of wine. How does a plate of spaghetti with a Coke sound?"

The same goes for finding the right technology solution. To pick the right solution, you have to take stock of your absolute necessities and then weight your "nice to have" items as they relate to your budget.

If you talk to five different vendors, they're going to offer you five different ways to solve your problem. Just because you choose one of them as the best solution for you doesn't mean the other four are bad products or service. They are just different ways to solve your problem and might not be as tailor made for your needs. It's okay if you don't pay for the seven-course meal (and it's okay if you do, as long as it makes sense for your situation).

It's important to know your own needs and wants very well, because salespeople are taught to "sell the sizzle." Tech demos are designed to push the "wow" factor for a product or service, but to use another metaphor, you don't walk into a Cadillac dealership to buy a new Escalade if your budget can only support a used Honda Accord with 35,000 miles on it. The Honda will still get you where you need to go, and it'll do it without the unnecessary spending.

Along with knowing your budget, the pandemic taught us an important lesson: look at tech solutions holistically. The CIO of one of my best customers called me in February 2020 and said, "I've done everything I can to beef up my corporate network and data center environment, but what happens when a hundred million people move to work-from-home environments using residential best effort ISP networks?"

At the time, it was eye-opening to me. I hadn't thought much about all of the changes that were happening so quickly around us in the early weeks of the pandemic. Everything was all speculation, all what if scenarios. So many people were having to embrace more robust security because the bad guys went into "beast mode" during the pandemic as they attempted to hack people working at home. Security at your home is historically nowhere near as good as your corporate office, and the bad actors knew that and exploited that for their gains.

Many companies had budgeted and built out VPN infrastructure to commonly support 20 to 25 percent of their workforce, but now they needed the infrastructure for 100 percent. The pandemic crushed anyone who hadn't adopted a cloud strategy. Indeed, we were slammed between March and early summer trying to help customers transition securely to work from home.

Spending for UCaaS (unified communications as a service), CCaaS (contact center as a service), Cloud, VPN, Multi-Factor Authentication, and other service solutions skyrocketed in 2020, and much that spending hadn't been in the budget for companies going into 2020. Business leaders were reacting desperately to try to maintain operations, and this often meant robbing Peter to pay Paul. As they looked frantically for solutions, many of them wound up being talked onto buying Cadillacs by persuasive salespeople, whether they needed them or not.

To avoid that, you have to understand the range of options in each category of technology that you're looking to buy. Let's consider a few key tech solutions.

Phone Systems

The old key phone systems were like workhorses. They easily kept going for fifteen to twenty years, and they were well-known for having lots of programmable buttons that you could use. These old phone systems were very popular with doctors and dentists, especially because they had park features that allowed you to put one call on hold while continuing a conversation with another. As the physicians moved from room to room, they could easily pick up a call on "park two" as opposed to having to go to their physical office to take a call.

Newer phone systems still have programmable buttons, but not nearly as many. Indeed, they often replace the buttons with web-based collaboration tools that can accomplish even more from a computer. However, it's important that you know how you prefer to use phones when you're going through the evaluation process. Do you want buttons, or are you okay clicking and dragging things on a computer screen? Are you getting all of the features that you need?

There's nothing worse than getting to the day of deployment and having an employee come to you and say, "Where are the park buttons?" I mentioned that story earlier. It happened to a medical center, and not having park buttons was obviously a huge problem for them. Figuring out that they didn't have park buttons on the day they deployed their fancy new phone system was a nightmare.

Contact Centers

I'm old enough to remember what it was like to sit on hold for forty-five minutes to talk to a representative on the phone about something. The younger generation has more of an immediate gratification mindset, and they are quickly becoming the largest consumers of products and services.

This has contributed to the transition from call centers to omni-channel contact centers, where you can meet your customers where they want to be met. These systems tend to incorporate phone, chat, SMS, and social media, allowing for quicker engagement and resolution. Data dips can reach into your system to capture previous purchases and buying trends which can help customer service reps make recommendations. Additionally, chatbots have replaced the self-search FAQs which were usually buried on the website somewhere.

Of course, just because a vendor has a contact center doesn't mean it's going to be perfect for you. Some of the newer breed of contact center solutions incorporate AI into their platforms so they can rate calls by words, phrases, and voice inflection. This enables them to coach reps with screen prompts, and also allows them to route potentially upset customers to the most experienced reps in order to improve the customer experience.

When customizing a contact center solution to meet your specific needs, features, reporting, and integrations will all play an important role. One size does not fit all, so make sure you know what features are available, which of them you need and would use in your everyday world, and if they will fit into your budget.

Backup and Disaster Recovery

Let's face it. We live in a world of server crashes, hard drive failures, and aggressive hackers. Backup and disaster recovery have never been more important. Twenty years ago, my wife worked for a small insurance agency, and one of her jobs was to take home the backup tape with their data every day. Now, backups happen automatically.

When it comes to investing in a backup service, the cost is usually related to how much data you want to back up, with a cost per terabyte of data. Disaster recovery focuses primarily on *recovery time objective* (RTO) and *recovery point objective* (RPO). RTO is the amount of time a business has to restore its processes at an acceptable service level in order to avoid intolerable consequences during a disruption. RPO, on the other hand, refers to the maximum amount of data that can be lost before significant harm is done to the business.

A cheaper disaster recovery service is probably going to offer a daily RTO backup and RPO data preservation after twenty-four hours. Whereas, a more expensive service might offer RTO backup every fifteen minutes and RPO data recovery in fifteen minutes. However, you also have to take into account egress fees. AWS and Azure are the two most popular public cloud solutions in the world. They are both easy to use, relatively cheap, and easy to set up. If you just need a cheap place to park your data, they work fine.

However, if you need to get your data back, they're going to charge you egress fees. If you're only transferring 40mb of data, it's not a big deal. However, if you need to transfer 200 terabytes, it could cost you thousands of dollars. In the event of a hack or ransomware attack, the biggest part of remediation is access to your data. There are vendors out there who will offer backup services without egress fees, so it's worthwhile to do your homework. Otherwise, you might make a costly mistake.

Cloud Services

The term "cloud services" is fairly vague, but it generally refers to any application or service that doesn't physically "live" in your office. Many people think cloud services are all the same, but that is far from true. First, you have public cloud services like AWS, Azure, and Google, which are multi-tenant shared environments. Then you have private cloud services, which are dedicated environments that serve a single organization. Some companies adopt a hybrid option, using a mixture of public and private services in their overall cloud strategy.

Bear in mind, a public cloud services is going to be quite cheap, while a private cloud service will be significantly more expensive. A hybrid solution will end up somewhere in the middle.

Networks

When it comes to networks, you have three basic options to choose from: good, fast, or cheap. You can pick a maximum of two, but you can never have all three. If you pick cheap and fast, you're going to get low quality. If you pick good and fast, you're going to pay a lot. The choice is up to you.

Just remember, as the need for cloud services increases, the need for bandwidth grows exponentially. Look at how much more bandwidth companies use today than they did ten years ago. This comes at a cost. A business that funnels their entire business cloud operations over a single broadband connection is asking for trouble. For that reason, dual connection networks running multiprotocol label switching (MPLS) and broadband in a primary/backup configuration are quickly being replaced by companies deploying SD-WAN, which uses both circuits for an "always on" solution.

At the same time, 5G is becoming mainstream for wireless, so vendors are sunsetting 3G technology. DSL and other copper-based solutions are being put out to pasture by the major telecommunication companies. Broadband fiber solutions, such as Verizon FIOS, AT&T ABF, and Lumen Fiber+ have become lower cost options for synchronous bandwidth than the asynchronous solutions provided by cable companies, and network services are available now on a building-by-building or region-by-region basis.

SD-WAN

SD-WAN, or *software-defined wide area network*, is a rapidly growing technology that is well-suited for the growing band-width needs of cloud-enabled organizations. It allows for lower cost deployments because VPNs can be put on multiple lower-cost connections.

The general idea behind this technology is to have multiple connections plug into an SD-WAN appliance that pings each circuit frequently and routes traffic to the best-performing provider. The end user can prioritize the traffic that is most important so the appliance knows what traffic to send where. Video and audio, in particular, can't tolerate latency, jitter, or packet loss, so an SD-WAN appliance will route them automatically to the best-performing route.

While all SD-WAN solutions will accomplish the routing strategy, they are not created equal. Indeed, there are many SD-WAN providers. Some of them choose to go to market directly as over-the-top solutions, while others focus on going through carriers as part of a managed network solution that integrates with firewalls. Additionally, some are packet-based, meaning the session can be placed over multiple links simultaneously, but others are session-based, meaning the application session runs on one circuit or the other.

Why do all of these differences matter? Let's supposed you're a large medical practice, and your inbound contact center is fielding appointment setting calls from across the country. Or maybe you're a financial services firm handling time-sensitive trading and market-based transactions. In both cases, a packet-based solution will send traffic across multiple connections simultaneously, so if a network incident occurs, the call with your patients won't drop and the financial transaction will always go through.

On the other hand, if you use a session-based solution, the patient would have to call back, and the trade would fail to complete, which could put your firm on the hook financially for the trade. In addition to the differences in how traffic is routed, you also have to consider your organization's ability to manage traffic by yourself. Some organizations want the transparency of using an over-the-top SD-WAN solution to manage their downstream network providers, but they have the people and skill set to handle everything in-house. Other organizations prefer to have the network provider handle it, while giving them visibility into everything so they can request changes when needed.

Know Thyself

With all of these different technology solutions, the wide range of options make it vitally important to understand your specific wants and needs. As you can see, all solutions are not created equal, and unless you find something tailored to your situation, you might wind up spending a lot of money just to get a whole lot of frustration.

If you lack the time or know-how to whiteboard your own wants and needs in light of your budget, then it would be wise to find a vendor-neutral advisor who can guide you in that process. But remember, you must always be looking to the future, because things change, and your solution must be able to change with you.

CHAPTER SIX

SCALABILITY AND FUTURE PROOFING

"If you fail to plan, you are planning to fail"
— Benjamin Franklin

Would you invite your divorce attorney to your wedding? That would be absurd, of course, and probably bring the wedding to a screeching halt. However, when you're looking to make a purchase of technology, whether hardware or software, you should make sure you have portability so you can shift that purchase to another underlying platform if you need to down the road. The concept can be difficult to grasp, but it's an idea that will serve you well in the long run. It goes back to the idea of thinking beyond the transaction.

Things happen. Circumstances change. Acquisitions are common. For example, a certain small networking company that was a vendor of mine got bought by a large, publicly traded company. It has been the worst experience of my professional career—five abysmal years of watching a company lose its way. When they were a small, independent business, they were the best in their field, but all of that has changed.

As soon as the new leaders came in, they said, "Oh, we've got our own way of doing things." And they proceeded to change all of the company's processes and systems. Suddenly, all of these customers who had started working with them based on my recommendation are looking to escalate their problems because they're upset with the changes. Many of them signed contract for services with the smaller company, and now they find themselves locked into those contracts after the company has been bought and changed for the worst.

Stuck in a Service

A similar problem can happen when you buy solutions on premise. You invest in the hardware and software, but before you know it, you've outgrown the solution and you have to buy more. I've seen companies invest in phone systems, buy equipment that is proprietary, and when they realized they were unhappy with the provider, they found they were stuck. The service wasn't portable to another vendor.

These kinds of things happen all of the time. I find myself warning people constantly, saying things like, "Beware, Company A doesn't play nice with anyone else. Company B is a little bit better but if you decide to use another service, you will have to upgrade to switch to another vendor"

Indeed, the cost of switching to another service provider can discourage companies from making changes that they need to make. If you've invested $50,000-$60,000 into a phone system, it's frustrating to have to pay over $100 per phone to make it work with another vendor. There's nothing more irritating than making a big investment in some tech solution only to discover that what you bought isn't best for you, or you've outgrown it, but you can't readily change to something else.

Outgrowing a service is a common problem, but it can go the other way as well. Companies can invest in a solution and then downsize and realize they need something a smaller and more affordable. There are so many variables at play that it's imperative that you do business with vendors who are going to be flexible if you need a change. At the end of the day, you are committing that you will stay with a vendor for a certain period of time (or a contract value) and they guarantee you a certain price. There are business downturns and some other creative language that can be put into contracts that help account for changes in your business that you can't predict at the time of the contract signing.

At the time of this writing, I'm right in the middle of a situation where what became important to the customer changed after the fact. We were helping a company find the right phone system, and as we went through the sale, we did all of our due diligence—the mobile app was merely a box to be checked. Prior to 2020, there were other things about the system that were way more important to them, but during the pandemic, the mobile app became more important. So, as we looked for replacement options, it seems reasonable that they should be able to test a solution ahead of time. They agreed.

Traditionally, you don't get to use a mobile app until further down the sales cycle, but we didn't want to waste our time or the customer's by choosing a solution only to find that the app didn't perform as they needed it to. To prevent this, we approached four different vendors and requested free proofs of concept for the customer. It was like a "try before you buy" scenario. Then, we took five users and had them download the apps and test them out for a week. This enabled us to find the app that worked best for the client, rather than simply jumping in with the first vendor who came along at the best price While this may not be an earth-shattering tactic, it's a logical approach that achieves an improved outcome.

Getting vendors to think outside of the box took some convincing, but in the end, it all worked out for everyone.

You probably won't get multiple options to test out if you approach a vendor by yourself. It's not standard operating procedure for a sale. You'll only get the opportunity if you work an independent agent because someone has to manage the process with no ulterior motives other than to find you the best solution.

With other customers, we have tried to talk them out of purchasing brands or devices that aren't portable enough to accommodate the unknowns of the future. With a couple of exceptions, Avaya and Mitel phones aren't typically portable to other services, so while both are solid solutions by themselves, selecting them brings limitations to future changes (that can only be corrected with costly changes).

Recently, both Avaya and Mitel entered into agreements with Ring Central to move to the cloud for hosted VOIP, which helped. Polycom and Yealink have taken a different approach because they want to work with virtually every hosted VOIP platform on the planet. Add in the Microsoft Teams element, and the water really gets muddied. Even though Teams-certified phones come from Polycom or Yealink, most of them won't work with other hosted solutions except Microsoft. But how could you know this if you don't live it day in and day out? And at $150 to $250 per phone, choosing incorrectly could prove to be very costly both financially and in mental frustration cost.

Evolving with You

Finding the right solution doesn't just mean finding a service that works for you now; it also means finding a service that can change and evolve along with you in the future. I've seen too many companies wind up regretting their purchases down the road when their needs evolved. It's the dreaded buyer's remorse syndrome.

This kind of thing happens all the time, and somehow the old RFP process doesn't prevent it. A vendor may not tell you that their server will create scalability problems for you in two years—not because they're trying to be deceptive, but because they're trained to promote the benefits and advantages of the product. You can go all-in on storage space, computing power, and software, but if you don't plan accordingly for your growth, you might find yourself outgrowing that physical box. Then you have to add another one. And another one. You have to keep spending large sums of money to add more stuff to keep up with your growth.

If you'd known all of your options beforehand, you might have been able to invest in a cloud-based solution that allowed you to scale without running into a bottleneck. The same thing happens with bandwidth. You might buy access at a 100mb and within no time you find that you're pegging a 100mb easily. Suddenly, you're dealing with a massive bottleneck in your traffic.

When you go to upgrade your service to a gig, you discover it's going to take forty-five to sixty days. That's a long time to deal with traffic jams, and potentially a lot of frustrated customers. All because you didn't anticipate how much your need for bandwidth would grow.

Portability, scalability, and future-proofing all have to be taken into consideration when seeking *any* tech solution. A vendor isn't necessarily going to warn you about these things when you approach them to explore their specific solution, and if you don't understand the competitive landscape, then you might wind up investing in a solution only to outgrow it before you've even paid it off.

Direct reps for a vendor is incentivized to try to make the sale regardless of whether something else might be better for you. Again, I don't say this as any sort of accusation against sales reps. As I said before, selling their product or service is how they get paid and support their families. It's what they're trained to do, and in most cases, they sincerely believe in the superiority of their company's solution. If they didn't believe in the quality of their company, I would argue they need to look for a new job. Still, if you outgrow the product you bought from them three years later, they're going to be long gone.

What's the alternative? Instead of going through an entire RFP process and approaching vendors directly, use a trusted technology advisor who can guide you through the decision-making process to a solution that won't hinder your growth or evolution as a company. Of course, all advisors are not created equal. You need someone who has the right amount of visibility into what the market is doing, someone who can do research themselves or has access to deep knowledge about available solutions.

Do such advisors exist? Of course, they do. Let's take a look.

CHAPTER SEVEN

TRUSTED TECHNOLOGY ADVISORS VS DIRECT REPS

"All great leaders choose great advisors,
people they really trust…"
— Tom Payne

See I've been both a direct rep *and* a trusted technology advisor at times during my career, and I can say from experience that they are both completely different roles. Direct sales is heavily reliant on quotas, which you either hit your number or you pack your bags. I had a boss at LCI who told me, "When you are at your quota, I work for you. When you are not, you work for me."

When I was a direct rep, I remember pushing hard to close a deal at 6:30 pm on New Year's Eve. Closing it at that time did no good for the customer. I couldn't even process the order yet. It only helped me because it ensured that I made a booking before the end of the year. While I was having a great year, but I hadn't met my quota for the month, so it was in my best interest to get that deal closed before midnight.

That's just the way it goes when you're a direct sales rep. Your motto is, "Close the deal and move on." Or more like the old quote from the movie *Glengarry Glen Ross*: "Only one thing counts in this life! Get them to sign on the line, which is dotted…Always. Be. Closing."

That's how you make money. That's your job! Consequently, most direct compensation models aren't geared around long-term satisfaction. They are transactional, and reps are incentivized to close as many deals as they can as fast as they can.

They usually get a one-time payment for a sale, or a payment tied to a short window where they can ramp up. After that, their compensation is done with that customer, and the customer is transferred to a customer service person in another department. Even then, those customer service reps are sometimes incentivized to get off the phone as quickly as possible—if the customer can even find a number to call in the first place. Good luck going to a big corporation website and finding a toll-free customer service number.

Increasingly, large companies want customers using chatbots, forums, and FAQs because they don't consume human resources. That frees them up to focus on closing deals, because again, that's the way you make money with a transactional approach.

I've experienced this myself. When I was in the process of buying Salesforce as a CRM, the sales rep acted like my best friend, but as soon as I closed the deal and made the purchase, he would no longer return my calls. He went from being my best friend to ignoring my calls the second money changed hands. Not all vendors are this way, of course, but it happens often enough to be a source of frustration for many people. I learned my lesson and hired a specialist for my current CRM and I could not be happier with the result.

However, a trusted technology advisor is the opposite. Trusted technology advisors are incentivized to create custom solutions for the client, and their income is largely based on residual compensation. If they don't give good service to a client, the client leaves, and so does their compensation. If a client leaves, an advisor gets nothing, so it behooves them to do their best work to find the right solutions that will keep that customer happy. Increasingly as solutions have become more complex over the years, and the front end heavy lift or infrastructure audit has required much more time, it's not uncommon for Trusted Technology Advisors to also have Project Based solutions as well. That is money well spent.

An advisor's job is to take a client through the journey and make sure they get the right tools and resources they need. When it comes to the RFP process, they help craft the scope of work from a vendor-neutral position using a whiteboard approach that help the client figure out what's important to them, and they invite all of the stakeholders to the table.

Let's suppose you have a contact center and you're looking to upgrade. To begin the RFP process, a trusted technology advisor will bring in the supervisors *and* the people who do the day-to-day work, as well as the team members who do analytics and create reports. Anyone who has a stake in this will discuss the scope of the work together. It won't just be the CIO making a decision and telling the contact center supervisors, "Make this work."

Then the advisor will look at multiple vendors and, working together with the clients, will score each of the vendors based on the suitability of their solution. In the end, they will be able to create a very short list of vendors that can be brought to the next stage of evaluation. It's a consultative and solution-based approach to helping a client. This isn't a direct rep pushing someone toward a transaction in order to close a deal.

Our Process: Reverse Engineered Decisions

When we work as a trusted technology advisor, we work with clients to come up with the scope of work for their RFP that determines their absolute "must haves" and "nice to haves." Once we come up with what they really need, we use software tools to identify vendors based on their *true* capabilities who can meet the client's criteria. We look at everything: their integrations, features, compliance, geography, and more.

Most importantly we *only* invite vendors who can check off all of those boxes so clients don't have to waste time responding to vendors who can't actually meet all of their needs. It's a bit like a pre-approval process for vendors. If you've ever bought a house, you remember how you got pre-approved by a lender up to a certain amount for your home loan? If you were pre-approved for a $500,000 loan, you wouldn't waste time looking at a $750,000 home, would you? We do something similar with these vendors.

Only vendors who meet all of the client's criteria are invited to the table. This streamlines the process tremendously and enables us to reverse engineer a solution customized for the client. We also involve vendor-agnostic sales engineers to work on bids. This is important because if you use, let's say, an AT&T sales engineer, they're going to talk about AT&T capabilities. However, if you use vendor-agnostic sales engineers, they're going to talk about the overall solution and have a deep understanding of key vendor differentiators. These differentiators are just about the most powerful pieces of information because they allow vendors to get included or excluded fairly quickly based on the boxes they check.

We can then ask the sales engineer a series of questions like the following: "What does this solution look like? What do the integrations look like. What type of firewalls do we have to integrate with? Do we want a session-based or packet-based service?" And so on. That sales engineer doesn't have loyalty to any particular vendor so they're going to look across all of our solutions to find the right one.

Of course, we're not the only ones who do this. I don't mean to suggest that we're the only trusted technology advisors on the market who can help you find the best solution. I only use our example as a way of revealing the real value of using a trusted technology advisors rather than interacting with direct sales reps. However, if you'll permit just a little bragging, I will say that we have access to some powerful tools that give us the ability to invite only the best vendors to the table. By using next-generation systems, vendor-agnostic people, and a proven process in a specific sequence, we get the secret sauce that is the RFP Alternative Process.

No more relying solely on your gut or trusting vendors to be honest about their ability to meet your needs. By using software tools and vendor agnostic engineering resources to identify the best possible vendors for your specific needs, it becomes far easier to reverse engineer a solution.

To be fair, there's nothing we talk about in this book that you couldn't theoretically do on your own, but it would be very costly, there would be a steep learning curve, and take a great deal of time to build out these robust resources. However, you have the option of using a trusted technology advisor who already has a bunch of powerful tools at their fingertips. It's an option that is worth considering. Would you rather approach twenty-five vendors and interview them to see if they meet your criteria, or would you rather work with an advisor who has the process to narrow that down to just five vendors who are the best fit from the beginning? Do you want to chase vendors down and research their capabilities or do you want pre-vetted vendors brought directly to you? I believe we've built a better mousetrap.

The Power of Pay-for-Performance

One of the most powerful aspects of working with a trusted technology advisor rather than approaching direct sales reps is that advisors are "pay for performance." They get paid to deliver results, save you time, promote efficiencies and get you to the best solution as painlessly as possible. And because they're not driving toward a singular transaction, they can begin providing value for a client right out of the gate.

Trusted technology advisors help ensure enhanced customer support between clients and vendors. The customer service game can feel a bit like playing hot potato, where the rep seems like they're in a big hurry to get you off the phone or transfer you to someone else as fast as possible. Sometimes, it's more like ping pong, where you've getting bounced between departments.

With a trusted technology advisor, this is no longer the case. You have choices that you don't have with direct reps. With Trusted Technology Partners you have an advocate in your corner who works with the vendor on your behalf if that is the way you prefer. Other customers prefer to work directly with the vendor, and we play more of an oversight role, ensuring expectations are met. Dedicated support people are there to manage the customer service experience because they are committed to your long-term success, no matter which option you feel best suits your business needs.

Often, as in our case, a technology advisor has lines of communication to the executive VP level of customer support. If a customer needs a response from customer service, I will personally use that line of communication in a heartbeat. I'd much rather ask for forgiveness than permission, even if that means leaping over layers of escalation.

As you may know from experience, when you try to escalate on your own, you're sometimes left hanging as the company reps wade through red tape to get approval to move you up the chain. I've had to deal with the red tape myself in the past. Indeed, the biggest and most successful companies can be the worst at this. It's one reason I've often preferred to work with small to midsized vendors. As long as they have the service and can provide what a client needs, they tend to be more nimble: less red tape and easier to get hold of a living, breathing human who can impact the change we are looking for to solve the problem.

Indeed, a vendor at a big company once told me, "Trying to change something at our company is like trying to make a U-turn on a cruise ship." Some companies are so big, they can't even get out of their own way, so when you're trying to escalate a problem or deal with an order, the *process* can get in the way of your *progress*.

With many companies, the bigger they are, the more complicated it becomes to deal with them. At the same time, as I told one vendor multiple times, "When everything you do requires an escalation, you're doing it wrong."

By using a trusted technology advisor, all of these complications are over with. You no longer have to put up with the ping pong customer service games or the layers of red tape. You'll never again have to hunt through webpages, desperately looking for a toll-free number that will lead you to an actual human being. You won't have to worry about being tossed aside as soon as you close the deal.

You'll never say, "Yesterday, that sales rep acted like she was my buddy. She really put me at ease and made it easier to sign the contract! Today, she won't take my call or respond to my email, even though I have a serious question about the contract. Did she drop off the face of the earth?"

If I sound like I favor the channel approach over the direct sales model as it relates to delivering the best technology outcomes to customers – BINGO!!! I think it's a better model all day long and twice on Sundays. It's like having a highly trained specialist as an extension of your business that is not a W2 employee. It's simply a better way to buy.

And when it comes to your RFP, a trusted technology advisor is committed to streamlining a process that will get you to your best solution as quickly and painlessly as possible, without ever trying to sell you something you don't need. Not a bad deal.

CHAPTER EIGHT

THE COACH APPROACH

"Selecting the right person for the right job
is the largest part of coaching."
— Phil Crosby

have fourteen years of coaching experience with competitive soccer up to the high school level. I coached some baseball as well, but Maryland is lacrosse land, so my son's interest changed. Coaching has taught me a few important lessons about helping customers get to their best solution. The first thing I've learned is that you need to understand what's important to all of the stakeholders. Learn what makes them tick, what they're good at, and what they need help with. Figure out how they all come together.

On a soccer team for example, the goalkeeper is a very single-minded person. They have one primary job, and as the last line of defense, they have to have a certain one-track defensive mindset. They also need to have the Etch-A Sketch mindset to be able to quickly forget when goals or flurries of goals can get into your head. To be a good coach for your goalkeeper, you must understand their role, their mindset, and how their job connects to the other players on the team. The same goes for every player and every position. A good coach understands every player and position and has a clear sense of how they work together.

Often, soccer coaches will take the fastest kid, put them up front, and say, "Go score goals." However, our team was trying something a little different. We decided to put all of the kids on the soccer field and throw a ball right into the middle of them. No positions were assigned; we just let them go at it. Then I stood back and watched to see who naturally gravitated toward each position.

At first, it looked like the blob that is five-year-old rec soccer: a swarm of kids in a pile with a bouncing ball in the middle. Eventually, they started spreading out, and I could see the protectors (defenders), the transition players with great footwork and passing skills (midfielders), and the kids who had a knack for creating goal-scoring opportunities (attack).

The father of a kid who gravitated toward defender approached me and said, "Hey, let my kid score goals. He's fast!"

But I told him, "He's best at defense. It's where he goes naturally when I throw the ball out there. He's a protector. Let him do what he does naturally. He's great at it."

It's the job of a coach to observe these things and make the most of them for the sake of the team. That approach has served me well as an advisor in the business world. Understanding what is important to each stakeholder and being able to communicate it to all of the other stakeholders in a way that makes sense is a valuable skill to have. It's not something everyone can do.

Indeed, in our space, there are many tech-minded "geeks" who are brilliant, but they can't speak outside of their own mindset. When they attempt communicate with other stakeholders, everything they say is accurate, but it's very high level. That said, we are very fortunate to have access to a great number of engineering resources who have a real gift for taking extremely complex technologies and breaking them down so everyone can understand them.

Before we had access to all the independent engineering

resources, we relied on the vendors themselves, but we still managed the process. We were in a meeting one time with a large company where we invited the final three vendors in a large network bid to do one final dog-and-pony show. We ordered lunch and gave the vendors a chance to explain why they should be the final choice, and the customer could then ask them additional questions face-to-face.

The rep I was working with brought in his sales VP and an engineer. The sales VP walked in forty-five minutes late, and the engineer was a complete disaster. He was, no doubt, a very intelligent man, but his customer-facing skills were a dumpster fire. The vendor left, and as I was helping clean up the conference room, I looked at the IT director and said, "I hope you enjoyed lunch, but they are off the prospective vendor list."

He smiled and replied, "I'm glad you saw it the same way I did."

The sales VP called me the next day and raved about what a great meeting it was, but I politely told him that I wanted whatever he was smoking because the meeting had been a disaster. I advised him that the engineer, who was clearly a very intelligent man, should never put on a suit and go in front of a customer again if they ever wanted to win a network deal again.

Thinking back on that meeting and the rough dynamic between the customer and the engineer, I am so thankful that we have access to such brilliant engineering resources who thrive in front of customers.

You need to be able to break down what each stakeholder values into common sense talk that helps everyone understand what the company as a whole needs. I call this the "coach approach." It's the ability to see and understand the different segments of a business, to understand how a solution will impact each of them, and to communicate this to everyone.

With today's integrations, tech solutions touch more people than ever before. Take customer relationship management (CRM) software, for example. What's fascinating about CRMs is how they integrate tools that touch so many different teams throughout an organization, from sales and marketing to project management and customer satisfaction. It's like seeing the full customer life cycle through a single lens.

Nowadays, there are so many different things that are important to people, so it's important to figure out what each of them needs in order to find the best solution. The coach approach isn't about trying to sell a particular system. It's about trying to customize a solution that meets the needs of multiple stakeholders in the organization so that the whole organization wins.

I can't count the number of times I've seen a company go through an RFP process and invest in a solution only to discover after the fact that it didn't meet the needs of one particular stakeholder. Sometimes, that stakeholder wasn't even part of the RFP process, so they get a rude awakening during deployment. A coach helps to ensure this doesn't happen.

Better Decision-Making

So, what does the actual role of a coach look like during our RFP Alternative process? First, they gather relevant information about potential solutions in a purposeful manner and present it to you, whether that means demos, proposals, or white papers. Sometimes, when a company is trying to gather information in order to find a customized solution, vendors can hold things up. This becomes a problem if you're trying to be up and running by a certain date. A coach helps to bridge that gap and acquire the information you need to make an informed decision.

Then, once you've settled on a solution, a coach helps guide you and the vendor through the process of getting it all set up and working properly on time: from purchase to deployment and even beyond deployment. A coach doesn't just get you to a signature and then bow out. On the contrary, after the signature, they are just as involved as ever, working with the vendor and managing the process to ensure that deployment is swift, correct, and timely. Sometimes, the customer can be the cause of the holdup on a particular project. The coach has to be able to effectively communicate to the client the impact of the delay, how it affects the project deliverables, and professionally nudge them to get the project back on track. We call this "pleasantly persistent project management."

We have our own project management process built into our CRM system because, let's face it, vendor project managers aren't always the greatest. We build customized timelines into our project management tool to make sure deployment stays on target. This added layer of project management serves as another set of independent eyes on the project, helping to ensure good outcomes. In some cases, this first deployment might be the first engagement with a client. You only get one shot to make a first impression so we include that added layer to help make it a good one.

Indeed, while traditional RFP stops at procurement, our RFP Alternative process goes past the deployment and right on through to ongoing management. In a sense, we become an extension of your business to ensure the success of your new technology. We believe that part of the coaching process is just as important as helping you find the right solution. Managing technology solutions is a journey, not a destination, and deploying the new solution is just the beginning of that journey.

Just as important is the fact that a coach is vendor agnostic. They're not working for any vendors. They're working for you!

CHAPTER NINE

VENDOR AGNOSTIC

"Focusing on solutions fuels progress."
— Michelle Gielan

A solution that is specifically tailored to solving your problems, creating efficiencies, saving money, and improving production does not have to be tied to a specific vendor logo. As we referenced earlier, if you're a sales rep for AT&T, then your job is to sell your company's products, so AT&T is always going to be the right solution for a customer, whether it's really the best fit or not. That's just the way the vendor mindset works. Part of their job is to be fully bought in—to drink the Kool-Aid, so to speak.

However, to get to the right solution for you, it's important to work with someone who is, as we like to say, "vendor agnostic." In other words, someone who defines the solution first, then invites a select few vendors to prove their product or service can fit into that mold. The vendors who are invited to make their pitch are pre-approved after the solution has been created, so the company already has clarity about what they need.

This is a different mindset for RFPs than the way they are

traditionally approached: *Figure out how to solve the problem first, then match the vendor.* When we do this for clients, we have access to dozens of sales engineers, each with their own "swim lane." They focus on the solutions in detail.

For example, we have contact center specialists whose job is to understand everything about contact centers and the vendor options that are out there. They understand the differentiators between vendors, what they're best-suited for, and so on. This becomes incredibly important, especially when the project is complex, because it allows us to tailor a solution that precisely meets our client's needs.

This takes a massive burden off the shoulders of those poor souls who have to evaluate vendor responses to an RFP. Typically, reading through vendor responses is one of the most arduous parts of the RFP process because somehow you have to figure out the nuances of every vendor so you know whether or not to invite them to the next step of the process.

Under the old process, this is heavily based on speculation and guesswork. Who can possibly figure out the nuances of dozens of different vendors and their solutions? Actually, a vendor-agnostic advisor with access to experts who specialize in various kinds of tech, as well as an extensive amount of information and resources, can handle this with relative ease. We specialize in "not all X service is the same" and have the resources to show you which solutions is best for you and why.

Additionally, by working with an advisor, you don't have to manage the vendors directly to drive positive outcomes. Going back to the differentiators between direct reps and channel reps, I work directly with my channel vendors every day, and they're some of the best people I know. Our engagements with customers are hand in hand, driving the solution for the customer. If you deal with a direct rep, it's up to the customer to drive the outcomes.

Look at a list of companies that have the worst customer

satisfaction, and you'll find that most of them are technology vendors.[1] There's a reason for this and it's often because their process is broken. Close the deal quick, get the customer off the phone quick, self-help customer service, and high turnover could contribute to these frustrations. In fact, I think most people would agree that the service that the vendor supplies is not all that bad. It's the process of contacting them or solving billing problems that is the most frustrating. Ping pong is a game, not a customer service strategy.

Vendors are obligated to have a self-serving mindset, but honestly, anyone who goes into business has to be a bit self-serving. They have to want their own success. Heck, I want to be successful as an advisor. Of course, I do. Everyone has to make money, and a vendor does it by selling products and services. It's as simple as that. However, without the right guidance, that mindset can lead to problems, especially in the tech world.

With over 300 vendors in our portfolio, we can find the right match for virtually any tech scenario. While we may have an idea who some of the players will be, the RFP Alternative Process fine tunes it. Since I am in Maryland, I will liken it to one of Maryland's gems, the Preakness. On that day, the best horse will inevitably win the race. Our process ensures the best tech vendor will win the bid, and they all come from our barn, so to speak.

Questionable Tactics

I know of a small restaurant that was looking for a phone system. They called a certain multinational telecommunications conglomerate and talked to a sales rep who convinced them to buy something that they didn't want and couldn't even use if they

---

[1] https://www.statista.com/statistics/657936/companies-with-worst-customer-service-us/

wanted to. All the restaurant wanted to do was transfer from their small carrier, who was sunsetting copper DSL service they were using to provide their phone service. At most, they needed a handful of lines that they could have routed over their existing internet.

However, the vendor never even asked them about their infrastructure. He just sold them a service that the restaurant couldn't remotely support because their network couldn't handle it. He was pushing promos which did more harm than good.

Maybe the vendor pushed it hard because he was trying to earn SPIFF (sales program incentive funds) and just needed to sell a certain number of VoIP services to customers. Or maybe he was behind his quota for the month. Whatever the case, he talked that restaurant into buying a service they couldn't even support when all they needed were some basic services.

As you might expect, this caused all kinds of angst and problems for the restaurant, and their problems dragged on for months as they tried to reach some kind of resolution. It caused constant service interruptions that hurt their small business, and the salesperson who sold the system to them made himself scarce as soon as the contract was signed. The vendor rep likely got paid for a solution that ultimately never got successfully deployed.

It's an all-too-common problem: someone sitting in a call center selling a customer something that isn't in their best interest. I can't count the number of times I've seen this happen. Maybe it's happened to you.

But there's another common problem that I see. A company using an old, inefficient system is looking for a better solution, so they talk to a direct rep at a new vendor. They are talked into buying a shiny new solution that is supposed to make things better, but the vendor doesn't help them get rid of the old solution. Once the solution is deployed, the customer is on their own figuring out what to disconnect and how to disconnect it. Without someone guiding them, often nothing gets disconnected.

Suddenly, the company is paying for both the old solution *and* the new solution. Through audits, I've seen situations where this has happened three or four times to a company over the course of ten years. They have multiple generations of tech solutions, older and newer, all housed in the back room, and they're afraid to get rid of the old tech because they think it might shut everything down. Nobody wants to risk the potential backlash of pulling the plug on something so they do nothing.

Now, they have old tech that was replaced by new tech that was later replaced by newer tech, and all three generations of tech are being paid for. And the next vendor who comes along will gladly sell them another solution to add on top of it all. It's a giant mess, and it's the result of vendors who are focused on transactions rather than outcomes and relationships.

Many direct sales models don't embrace ongoing relationships as much as they are focused on transactions. A sales rep is incentivized to cultivate a relationship with you as long as it moves you through the sales cycle, but as soon as you put your name on that DocuSign contract, the vendor must necessarily move on to the next prospective sale. That's why you get handed off to customer service, often time across the pond with some big vendors.

To be fair, sales can be hectic. You have to constantly try to move people down the sales funnel to be successful, so wasting time lingering in the post-sale period is harmful to your on-the-job performance. I remember this all too well during my years as a direct sales rep.

When I was a direct rep, I sold some solutions to a well-known clothier in my area, but it took over a year to cultivate the relationship. They were growing and they were a great name in the region so I went to finance and got aggressive with our pricing so we would win. We won it but back then we had to write the orders by hand, and eventually, the stack of orders was over a foot tall, and my hand was cramped for weeks.

Shortly after the solutions were installed, the customer contact asked me to meet with him so we could go over everything. He wanted me to help him clean up the billing from the old company. I agreed and wound up spending an entire afternoon with him, but I was happy to do it. After all, I had just made a nice chunk of change from this company's order.

When I got back to the office, I received a severe tongue-lashing from my regional sales director, who accused me of wasting the whole afternoon with the client. "It's a waste of time if there's no immediate new business to get from them," he said.

"But they're adding twenty to thirty new locations per year," I replied.

"That's what account managers are for," he shouted.

I remember walking out of his office ticked off. I was the number one sales rep in the Mid-Atlantic due in large part to this company's order, and my regional sales director had just ripped me a new one for spending time with them. To be fair, he wasn't technically incorrect, especially under that sales model, but it didn't sit well with me.

People are oversold solutions far too often. It happens to my own clients all the time. Vendors approach them and try to sell them stuff that they clearly don't need, and I have to warn them about it. A large infamous company (that shall go unnamed) contacted one of my clients recently and said, "Hey, we've got this new security suite and backup solution that you should know about." And before my client could take a breath, they jumped right into a hard sell.

The vendor never once asked my client if they needed the solution, if they already had security software or a backup solution. Indeed, the customer already had both. They had a firewall through a managed service provider (MSP) and a secondary circuit. They didn't need another security suite, and the backup solution was unnecessary. The vendor knew none of this, didn't ask, and quite frankly, probably didn't care. He just needed to make a sale.

One of the things many sales people do too often is the good old-fashioned "feature dump," which usually happens before they even know what the customer's needs are. The sales rep will say something like, "Mr. Prospect, our solutions with XYZ Vendor solves Problem A, B, C, *and* D." They assume they know the customer's problems before asking, and while XYZ Vendor may indeed solve problems A through D, if the prospect doesn't feel like those are problem areas for them, the sales rep mark has been missed.

We choose to ask open-ended questions whenever possible because most business owners or operational leaders know what their challenges are and what pain points they cause for the company. Producing operational efficiencies is every bit as important as how much something costs.

And, of course, we're all familiar with some of the questionable tactics that are used by some service providers when it comes to pricing. For example, a vendor will sell a suite of products under a temporary bundle discount, but when the discount ends in six months or a year, suddenly the customer finds that their bill is 30 percent higher than they expected.

Some vendors aren't always clear about fees, surcharges, and price increases. In fact, they rarely talk about them at all. And tech companies that are regulated by the FCC have certain mandatory FCC fees that they charge and probably don't mention, including things like Universal Service Fund fees, administrative fees, and so on. So, a company will buy a service on a fixed cost, then discover all of the tacked-on fees when they get the first bill.

Many years ago, during my direct rep years, I sold MCI in a large call center with 400 other sales reps. I hated it. The room was filled with a sound like bees buzzing. As a rep, I prided myself on being reasonably intelligent and knowing our service and our competitors quite well. And then I got outsold by the guy next to me, who was as dumb as a box of rocks.

As it turned out, he would call people and say, "Congratulations! You have won a thousand dollars in free long-distance calling!" It worked, and he outsold me almost every month. I finally realized that my mindset was not well-suited to that environment. I naturally tended toward a highly-informed, consultative approach, and I tended to say things like, "Let's talk through this and see if it works for you."

I learned the hard way that the impersonal, nameless, faceless, one-call close environment of the sales call center was not my thing. When I realized this, it was like the writing on the wall: I loved offering technology solutions to customers, but I was in the wrong environment. However, as a trusted technology advisor, the consultative approach makes all the difference. We acquire all of the relevant information and bring it together for our client. We act as vendor management experts. And we advocate for the customer all throughout the RFP Alternative process.

To be fair, everyone has their strengths. The guy sitting beside me in the MCI call center knew how to close a sale very effectively, but I have learned that I'm more suited for taking customers through a different journey. Through my years at MCI and then LCI/Qwest, I gained just enough direct sales experience to realize I didn't want to be in it. Now, when I work with a client, my channel vendor reps represent their companies, and I represent and advocate for my clients and manage the information exchange process. We engage the right people when and where they are needed to build out the solution that makes sense. It's a beautiful partnership that gets people to the best solutions efficiently.

Why would a vendor work with someone like me when I am drastically narrowing down the number of people who get to approach and sell to a prospect? Simple. Because their model is to cast a wide enough net for people like me that they still hit their sales numbers.

Even though the vendor still has a number to hit, they are very clear about how we work and who we are. They know coming into the process that our job is to advocate for the customer and find the best solution for them, so they won't be trying to sell something that isn't a good fit. And, importantly, there won't be any sales gimmicks or tactics, just solutions that make sense. Our channel vendor reps are extremely professional and represent their vendors well to give them every opportunity for us to present them if they are the best fit.

I'm always transparent, open, and honest with vendors. I think that's only fair. They deserve to know what they're getting into. If they're not selected for a bid, they will understand why. Even though I'm an advocate for the customer, I want to have good vendor relationships as well. After all, they're part of helping the customer achieve success, too.

It's a balance. Sometimes, a vendor is a great person, but they're missing the mark on something for this particular project. Maybe their install fee is too high, or maybe something vital is missing from their solution like an integration. Whatever the case, I want to educate them on it so they can be better. Not only am I advocating for the customer, but I'm also helping the vendor to create more satisfied customers.

Every customer situation is a blank slate, so we let the process and customization dictate who will be selected. We may get down to the final two vendors only for a customer to say, "Who would you pick?" At that point, I try to give detailed pros and cons based on real-life experiences or an overview of which vendor's processes would be a better fit for the customer's way of doing business. Sometimes, if all things are equal, I might match the personalities of the support team with the customer to ensure the most positive experience.

Satisfaction Isn't Enough

To be clear, I'm ultimately fighting for the clients that I represent, but the way I see it, when vendors get better, everyone wins. Customer satisfaction is ultimately a rather low bar to strive for.

Why not go *beyond* satisfaction to give customers absolutely the best product or service on the market at a fair price?

Satisfaction is the floor. Let's reach for the ceiling. You can get satisfaction by walking into a room and hitting the light switch. The lights turn on, and you're satisfied. Unfortunately, that's the level many vendors in the technology space strive for. They have a product or service. They sell it to you. They hope you're satisfied with the sale. The end, everybody moves on.

But trusted technology advisors don't sell a single product or service. They represent dozens of services and they constantly push vendors to do better. We're always asking, "What else can you do to improve the solution for the customer? How could you innovate to make this even better?" Most of our vendors *want* that feedback because they want to improve the customer experience and win more deals from trusted technology advisors like me. In one instance one of my vendors was looking for a particular CRM integration. The solution was a great fit for one of my vendors, but they did not yet have the integration. They developed the integration, and now not only could they help this client, but they were better positioned to help other clients in that vertical. It was a win-win for everyone.

It's important to have someone who can think about these questions from a vendor-agnostic perspective, where they don't represent just one logo. This became even more important during the pandemic, as companies found themselves looking for solutions and taking on expenses that they hadn't needed in the past. Even beyond the pandemic, some tech products and services are bound to become more important and more expensive—data security, for example.

More than ever, companies need someone who can come in with no preexisting loyalties to a particular company, product, or service, look at everything, and find better and better solutions for customers. Someone who can say, "You're paying too much here. We can shift technology there. We can change this, improve this, remove this."

In recent years, major providers are eliminating all of their old copper landlines and replacing them with fiber, but some companies still need the old landlines. Think of alarm companies, for example, or the phones that are inside of elevators that you're not supposed to touch. They still use analog lines. With that technology being essentially eliminated, alarm companies, elevator companies, and others are forced to find vendors who can help them make the transition to a newer technology. VOIP and wireless devices are being deployed to replace the old copper solutions.

When you have to make a change like that, a change that perhaps you didn't anticipate or budget for, it can be exhausting to talk to eight or nine companies that provide solutions. As a vendor-agnostic advisor, we whittle that list down to just three vendors who provide solutions that are the best fit for the needs, wants, and budget of our clients. This makes it a whole lot easier to determine which solution makes the most sense. Another key differentiator is that we bring the solutions directly to you rather than you having to chase them down yourself.

Solve the need first, then reverse engineer the solution. That's our approach. Being vendor agnostic means striving for outcomes, not cheesy sales pitches. Solving problems with real solutions, not closing deals by any measure to whoever pays us the most. Cultivating relationships through quality information exchange and thoughtful questions, not meticulously managing pipelines.

My good friend Donny, who I spent time on the field with as a coach, used to tell his team, "If you do all the little things well, the outcome of the game will take care of itself." Positive outcomes are the result of solving problems and cultivating relationships, and when you do that well, everyone wins. To be fair, sales orders drive my business just like anyone else's, but a sale in my world is merely one stage in the journey. It comes *after* the front-end customization has been done for the customer and *before* the project management and ongoing enhanced support. Like Donny says, if we put in the work for the customer and cultivate the relationship, the sales orders will take care of themselves.

In the world of trusted technology advisors, there's an added bonus for a job well done. If we knock it out of the park for one project, such as a VOIP deployment, and the customer is happy, they will likely come back to us for contact center, SD WAN, security, wireless, data center, help desk, and all the other service options that we have in our portfolio. Our portfolio of vendors and service offerings is large for that very reason.

Perfect the way the customer evaluates technology solutions, do the job well, rinse, repeat. That's how we do it.

If you'll excuse a tiny bit of bragging, I have four trusted technology advisor certifications in the industry in 1) security, 2) backup and disaster recovery, 3) VoIP and unified communication (UCAAS), and 4) contact centers (CCAAS). Those certifications are about the industry, products, services, and value we bring to customers. They're also about how we take the customer through the process of finding solutions, the differentiators, the potential "gotchas." As new certification courses are built, I always try to be near the front of the line to go through the course. The better I am for my customers, the more value I bring to the relationship. I train my ass off so my customer's don't have to.

I share this only so you'll understand that there is some accountability for trusted technology advisors. Not everyone can do what trusted technology advisors do. So, when we sit down with a customer and begin to whiteboard their needs, we have a deep understanding of their industry and the particulars of their situation. If we work with a financial company, we know they're going to have compliance requirements. If we work with a medical company, we know they have to deal with HIPAA requirements. If we do business with the federal government or with companies who sell to the government, we know they have FedRAMP certification to deal with.

Every company's situation is different, so everyone's journey to a tech solution needs to be different. It's a trusted technology advisor's job to understand this and find the right path ahead for each company—without any unhealthy vendor loyalties or sales quotas that might influence them to push a customer in a direction that isn't best for them. That's "vendor agnosticism" and it makes a huge difference in our RFP Alternative process.

Now We Need a System

So, we've identified some key ways to improve the RFP process: using a trusted technology advisor who is vendor agnostic and has a coach approach, using a whiteboard to identify your specific needs and wants, streamlining vendor selection to a few pre-approved vendors, having a customer advocate who will deal with the vendor to find the best possible solution, and using vendor management to ensure successful deployment.

Now, we just need a unified system to bring all of these elements together.

CHAPTER TEN

A SYSTEM THAT BRINGS IT ALL TOGETHER

> "If you can't describe what you are doing as a
> process, you don't know what you're doing."
> — W. Edwards Deming

Imagine a perfect scenario, where the best and brightest IT and technology resources have been brought together to change the way people buy technology. Imagine the simplicity of Carvana combined with the validation of a Better Business Bureau and the guidance of a major consulting company like Deloitte—all in one package. Each of these is a great offering on their own, but when you bring them together, it becomes a real game-changer.

That's what the ProfitComm RFP Alternative process is like for technology and vendor evaluations. It's a process where the most complex technology vendor evaluations are done *for* you, with all of the differentiators laid out in front of you, so you can see all of the features, integrations, pricing, and ongoing support options clearly defined and summarized in a format that is easy to read and understand.

With the RFP Alternative process, you only have to interact with vendors who have been vetted and pre-approved, and you're working with a vendor management expert whose only goal is your happiness. Plus, you have access to tools that are specifically designed to help with decision-making across many technology segments. This is what we do.

At the time of this printing, we have access to more than 300 vendors in our portfolio, along with numerous subject matter experts and engineers to help guide you through solutions and walk you through what you need. There's a big difference between a want and a need, and your budget needs to prioritize the latter over the former, so it's important to clarify the difference. We define a need as "those things that produce value, generate revenue, and make your customers happy."

Ultimately, it's not just about replacing old technology. It's about being able to set the stage for the future while managing the present. As I alluded to earlier, we have even built our own CRM platform that provides a vendor project management tool to ensure the RFP Alternative process is clean. After all, anyone can select a new vendor, but you also have to protect yourself from a bad deployment. We didn't always have that project management system, but we saw over time that it was necessary to help our clients. We evolved to improve outcomes.

A bad deployment with new tech is something that's going to be ingrained in the minds of your customers for a long time, and they will talk about it. When that small restaurant's customers had trouble reaching them on their VoIP phone, they talked about it, and they went elsewhere for their meals. Customers talk about you when you're good, and they talk about you when you're bad. So, you want to deliver a good experience as often as you possibly can.

In the technology business, if something doesn't work, all hell breaks loose. Think about it. if your phone system goes down, it's chaos. If your cloud service goes down—as it did for many people not so long ago when Amazon Web Service crashed for many people on the East Coast—it's chaos. Suddenly, all of your cloud-based services are unavailable. This is a good way to lose a lot of business.

Everybody wants everything to be perfect, but we've earned some of our best relationships by rolling up our sleeves, getting in the trenches, and helping clients make things right. We don't hide behind voicemail or transfer clients from department to department. We make ourselves fully accessible and available, so clients can deliver products and services that are mission critical in their day-to-day business.

We're there from the evaluation process all the way to the post-sale period. Remember, it's not all about the sale or transaction for us. It's about the relationship. Or, put another way, it's a journey, not a destination. And when it comes to buying tech, you're rarely done when you're done. There are always going to be modifications or changes. We're there to take customers through the full life cycle, the long-haul approach. To prove it, my very first order when I started in May of 1999 was a multi-site frame relay order (yep, you read that right – frame relay, an old data network service). The customer's needs evolved and so did the technology over the years and we were there to help them through all of it. That customer is still doing business with me at the time of this writing in 2022.

There are plenty of people who will help you evaluate vendors, but usually, once you've made the sale, you're on your own. You're stuck having to manage deployment by yourself. We can help identify different types of deployments from self-installs to white glove professional roll outs. But we're there all the way through deployment and beyond no matter what you select. We offer ongoing support, and we hold vendors accountable so they do what they say they're going to do.

It's not just about confronting people when there are problems. It's also about encouraging them when things go right. The art of encouragement is a bit of a lost art. Sometimes, it's as simple as sending a vendor a note that says, "Hey, I really appreciate you going above and beyond for us."

I've been doing things like that since I was in direct sales many years ago. Back then, my company worked with a group of six to eight people in Ohio who processed orders all day long. I remember tracking down their birthdays and sending them birthday cards and thank-you cards throughout the year.

Some people in the company thought I was nuts for doing this, but it made a difference. My orders got prioritized, my customers installed sooner, and I got paid faster. The little things matter. I remember one woman in particular who worked for the order processing team telling me, "All of our people absolutely love you." There was a method to the madness, and in that scenario, it worked for me.

I try to do the same thing today. When vendors do well, I let them know. I show my appreciation in big and small ways. Sometimes, it's an e-mail to their manager. Comtel used to call them "kudos," and you could nominate someone for a kudo for going above and beyond.

In one instance, a hospital customer was having construction done on a Saturday morning when they hit a fire hydrant. Water flooded all the floors below, including their IT room where we were supplying them with internet on a managed router. We learned quickly that water and routers don't play well together.

I was out of town, but our support rep took the call and worked on it all weekend. Since it was an insurance job, he had to take additional steps to get approved, but he got the job done. He had a new router programmed and shipped by the vendor by Monday afternoon so service could be restored. I nominated him for a kudo right away, and he received acknowledgement and a bonus for going above and beyond. Right after that, I advised the customer that they might want to move their IT gear to higher ground.

That was one example of encouragement but there have been

many others. A quick e mail to someone's boss telling them how they took a bad situation and made lemonade from lemons. Our society is quick to complain and criticize but slow to give someone a "nice job." I don't want me or my company to be seen in this industry as a proverbial pain in the ass. Praise should be given. If the praise is for a job well done, so be it. If the job missed the mark, constructive criticism is best.

That stated, I'm there to advocate for my clients, and that means sometimes I find myself going head-to-head with a vendor to get clients what they need. Things can get pretty heated, but that's a commitment I make to my clients. They're not going to be left alone to deal with vendors, and I will do whatever I have to do on their behalf. Hopefully if we have chosen wisely with the selection process, those instances of difficult situations are few and far between.

But when a vendor goes above and beyond to deliver value to my clients, I make sure they know how much I appreciate them. Unfortunately, with the direct rep model, vendors are only policing themselves—or else the customer has to police them, which is tough if you don't know what the industry standards are. You end up having to act as a vendor detective, trying to figure out what the real differences are between who a vendor claims to be and who they *really* are.

With a trusted technology advisor, you have an industry expert who is also a vendor detective. They can clarify for you what the real differences are between vendors so you always know exactly what you're getting into. Can you imagine what a difference this makes through the RFP process?

The RFP Alternative Process in Action

So, what does this RFP Alternative process look like from beginning to end? Let's walk through it.

The first step of the RFP Alternative process is to use our tools to help a customer craft the detailed scope of work. To do that, we conduct a needs analysis. This is where we sit down with a whiteboard and talk to the client to determine what they need, what features are important to them, what compliance they have to have, and so on. Ultimately, we're answering the "who, what, when, where, and why" of their vendor evaluation. Key to this stage of the process is getting every stakeholder involved and making sure they each have a voice early in the process.

In some instances, we might need to engage vendor-agnostic and technology-specific experts to help us craft the scope of work. Once that's done, we identify the vendors who will be best able to meet the specific needs of the client, and we get in touch with them on the customer's behalf. Through direct calls and meetings with the vendors, we get all the relevant information to them. Then we deliver our RFP Alternative in a specific format that makes the most sense.

From there, we conduct demos of those vendors' solutions. In some cases, we might even use a proof of concept. We've created a rating system that touches on ten key items and we have the customer score each of them on a scale from one to ten.

It's all about trying to do the right thing by the customer. When we finally put the vendor financial proposals in front of the customer, they've each been rated for a number of factors, but every stakeholder gets a say in the rating process. Once we tally everything up based on all of the aspects of the vendor proposals that matter to them, the resulting scores usually speak for themselves.

Based on that score, we identify the top two or three vendor proposals and do a deeper dive on them, gathering all of the information that the client will need about each of them in order to feel comfortable engaging with them for the next three years and possibly beyond. We walk the client through the pricing segment and contractual elements, and we try to find contracts that are going to be advantageous to them. For example, many vendors put auto-renewal clauses in their contracts, so often we'll negotiate a non-renewal clause into the contract or we submit the non-renewal form with the original contract. Yes, we invite the divorce attorney to the wedding, so to speak.

We always conduct plenty of due diligence with vendors to make sure they can deliver what they promise for the client. That means looking at their inventory, processes, and more. After all, clients don't know what they don't know and our role is to guide them. In the end, the client will be able to make a choice from among that shortlist of vendor solutions with clarity and confidence in a fraction of the time it would take if they did it themselves. During the pricing exercise, we are in constant contact with the vendors, and they always ask us, "How do we look?" I tell them where they can be more competitive.

One such pricing exercise happened with a client when we did an RFP Alternative bid for their contact center. We were able to get the winning vendor down $94,000 after the initial pricing exercise over a three-year term by having them lower some seat pricing and change the pricing structure from named agent to concurrent agent. This model worked better for the client, and at their monthly spend rate, it was like getting four free months of service.

Then we make sure deployment is well managed. Remember, we're advocating for our clients constantly, managing the vendor and making sure that deployment goes well. Even beyond deployment, we continue to advocate with clients to make sure vendors keep their promises and obligations. With all of our vendors, we have escalation lists all the way up to the C-suite, because there's nothing worse than having a problem with a service and not knowing where to go to get it addressed.

Indeed, once we get through deployment, we have multiple contacts, including the account manager, customer service rep, and vendor reps. At no time will a client not know who to call (or be unable to reach someone) when there's a problem. Additionally, we strive to contact every client routinely to make sure everything is good. We want to know how they're doing, if the solution is still meeting their needs, and it also keeps us up-to-date on their changing situation.

That's the essence of the RFP Alternative process. It's an RFP that is better able to meet the needs of all relevant stakeholders, a streamlined process that only engages with a select few vendors who can clearly meet those needs, and a system of accountability and advocacy that uses experts and tools to ensure the right solutions are delivered and deployed correctly for the long-term success of the client.

CONCLUSION

"There is no greater harm than that of time wasted."
— Michelangelo

L et's face it, one of the biggest problems with the old RFP process is just how much time is wasted wading through vendor options trying to make an informed decision about which solution to purchase. And all too often, it's time wasted because you don't know what you don't know. That's why so many clients end up with solutions that aren't quite right, or can't grow and evolve with them to meet future needs.

Even when we're not helping clients, we are constantly gathering intel on industry changes so we can provide that information to clients. Nothing is more empowering than being educated and informed. When Amazon Web Services went down on the East Coast in 2021, we sent an email to all of our clients to make sure they understood what was happening and how it might affect them.

When a big telecommunications company had a major outage not long ago, we sent an email right away to all of our client so they didn't have to sit on hold with them for forty-five minutes trying to figure out what was going on. Beyond that, we're always looking for new ways to cut costs for clients or find ways that they can do things more efficiently. One of our clients is a medical practice, and they do nothing but call and confirm appointments all day. We recommended using an SMS platform, where patients could reply to a text with a simple yes or no. In the end, it was a huge game-changer for them.

You see, it's not just about selling and supporting a service. We view ourselves as an extension of our clients' businesses. To that end, we help them understand their own differentiators, what makes them tick, what makes them better than their competitors, and what their competitors are doing. If you learn that a competitor is using a certain app, maybe it will be a good fit for you, too.

There's real power in knowing yourself, knowing your industry, and knowing what vendors really have to offer. This is just part of what we provide for our clients. Above all, it's a technology consulting relationship. Clients get to pick and choose where and when they engage us as projects come along, but we make ourselves wholly available to them.

And when a client comes to us with a need, we take them through the journey, from needs analysis, to evaluation, to deployment and beyond. We go and find the best solutions and bring those solutions to them, which saves time, money, and headaches. Once they select a vendor, we manage the project to make sure the vendor does what they're supposed to. We take responsibility for holding vendors accountable to meet our expectations as well as the customers.

It makes a difference when you have someone in your corner all the time making sure you get what you need—a consultative relationship that isn't transactional. We do our homework and if something doesn't feel right, we plant our feet firmly and fight for our clients. As Captain America said once upon a time (if we can adapt it slightly), "Sometimes your job is to plant yourself like a tree beside the river of truth and tell the vendor, 'No, *you* move.'"

Our customers mean everything to us, and we are constantly striving to be better, to offer more value, to refine what's considered normal. To be fair, the RFP Alternative was born out of both successes *and* failures. The successes are easy—just do it that way over and over. But the failures, or learning opportunities, allow us to self-reflect and strategize for better ways of doing things.

I'd love to tell you that we've done everything 100 percent perfectly for twenty-plus years, but that wouldn't be honest. In reality, the RFP Alternative has evolved over time, and my promise to anyone who does business with me is that it will continue to evolve. I strive to be better trained, always learning, to always have my head on a swivel, and to always strive for better processes and outcomes in the ever-changing technology landscape.

We will continue to align ourselves with the right resources, vendors, and platforms to bring only the best solutions to your doorstep.

Doesn't that sound like a better way? What's your time worth?

For More Information

To learn more about our RFP Alternative process, or any of our other services, check out our website at http://profitcomm.com/ or contact me directly at 888.266.5575. I will gladly give you a demo of our process and tools so you can see for yourself how we help clients find the solutions they need. You see, I'm not interested in making empty promises. I would love for you to see our process in action for yourself, with no strings attached. Contact me today!

ACKNOWLEDGEMENTS

I would like to start by thanking Ben Humphreys of Comtel Communications for helping me start what eventually became my company in May of 1999. You have been a friend, a mentor, and a great partner. You saw something in a twenty-nine-year-old kid and gave me all the tools to build a life for me and my family. I will forever be grateful.

To the rest of the Comtel/Simplicity/ProfitComm team—Heather, Tami, Lenada, Larry, Amy, Pete, Mike, Patti, and Patrick—you always made my customers your top priority, and I thank you. I appreciate your friendship.

To my business coach and friend Erik Sauer, for keeping me honest, helping me strive towards the company vision, and chase fewer shiny objects. I tell people that what I like about our relationship is that you are my scale and my mirror, neither lie. What you built with *There Goes My HERO* is truly amazing, I'm proud to be a part of it, and I'm proud that my company supports the cause. Go to http://www.theregoesmyhero.org to see how HERO is savings lives.

To my Goldman Sachs *10,000 Small Business* coach Robin and the rest of the GS10KSB Baltimore Cohort 8, thanks for helping me shape the RFP Alternative story.

To Jeffrey Miller, thank you for helping me with the book. You've got a gift and I appreciate how easy you made the process.

To the many channel managers and partner dealers that I have had throughout the twenty-plus years, thank you for your support for me and my customers.

To Wayne Coffey, thanks for always being willing to listen, help, challenge me, and open doors for me as I was getting started. Thanks for introducing me to the non profit board world with NMSC.

To my referral partners and sub agents, there is no greater compliment you can pay me than to stake your reputation by bringing me to help someone who trusts you. I will never take that lightly and I value that trust and partnership.

To my mom and dad, I hope I make you proud.

And lastly to my wife Dawn, and my children Amanda and Ryan, you are the reason I wake up every day and work my tail off. You make me whole. I love you with all my heart.

REFERENCES

Info

https://www.webfx.com/blog/web-design/the-history-of-the-internet-in-a-nutshell/
https://lifeboat.com/blog/2019/10/public-internet-access-brief-history
https://thereboot.com/internet-evolution-a-timeline-history-of-the-network/
https://www.allconnect.com/blog/history-of-internet

Photo's

https://www.facebook.com/wearedevelopers/photos/a.1110562128959028/4088961374452407/?type=3
https://www.kaspersky.com/resource-center/infographics/stuxnet
https://www.cyberdefensemagazine.com/at-least-3-different-groups-have-been-leveraging-the-nsa-eternalblue-exploit-whats-went-wrong/
https://www.trendmicro.com/vinfo/pl/security/news/cyber-attacks/hacktivism-101-a-brief-history-of-notable-incidents
https://www.zajil.com/how-the-internet-was-invented-history-of-the-internet/

ABOUT PROFITCOMM

Established in 1999, ProfitComm is your vendor management expert. We help businesses evaluate, deploy, and manage tech solutions from hundreds of vendors and dozens of service lines.

We help businesses manage technology at a fast pace. Many businesses get frustrated and waste their time with poorly performing technology vendors. By engaging with ProfitComm, you benefit from our processes, resources, and experience. ProfitComm's RFP Alternative process was designed to save you time and headaches by improving your technology management outcomes.

We partner with over 300 of the industry's leading vendors to equip our clients with the latest technologies. Our success is rooted in our ability to deliver the most efficient and cost-effective solutions through an expansive network of partners, vendors, and equipment providers.

We passionately serve our customers to get them better experiences and outcomes. Our dedicated client services team and the local Baltimore support team provide a consistent customer service level and hold vendors accountable. ProfitComm's customers get a reliable customer service experience regardless of who the vendor is.